TRACING YOUR ANCESTORS
USING NEWSPAPERS
A GUIDE FOR FAMILY HISTORIANS

TRACING YOUR ANCESTORS
USING NEWSPAPERS
A GUIDE FOR FAMILY HISTORIANS

CHLOE O'SHEA

Pen & Sword

FAMILY HISTORY

First published in Great Britain in 2026 by
PEN AND SWORD FAMILY HISTORY
An imprint of
Pen & Sword Books Ltd
Yorkshire – Philadelphia

ISBN 978 1 03613 473 0

Typeset in 10/13.5 Palatino by SJmagic DESIGN SERVICES, India.
Printed and bound in the UK by CPI Group (UK) Ltd, Croydon, CR0 4YY.

The Publisher's authorised representative in the EU for product safety is
Authorised Rep Compliance Ltd., Ground Floor, 71 Lower Baggot Street,
Dublin D02 P593, Ireland.
www.arccompliance.com

For a complete list of Pen & Sword titles please contact

PEN & SWORD BOOKS LTD
George House, Units 12 & 13, Beevor Street, Off Pontefract Road,
Barnsley, South Yorkshire, S71 1HN, England
E-mail: enquiries@pen-and-sword.co.uk
Website: www.pen-and-sword.co.uk

or

PEN & SWORD BOOKS
1950 Lawrence Rd, Havertown, PA 19083, USA
E-mail: uspen-and-sword@casematepublishers.com
Website: www.penandswordbooks.com

CONTENTS

ACKNOWLEDGEMENTS

With many thanks to:

James O'Shea
Mum and Dad
Gaynor Haliday
Amy Jordan
My ancestors

Credit is also due to:

British Newspaper Archive
Findmypast
Midland News Association
KM Group
British Cartoon Archive
Coventry Archives
DC Thomson & Co Ltd
Birmingham Libraries

INTRODUCTION

To build our family trees, we gather names, dates and relationships and plot them as we go. We discover the places where their major life events took place and how old they were when they married, had children and died. As family historians, we soon realise that our family tree is about so much more than names and dates and trying to get as far back in time as possible. We discover that we want to know who our ancestors were.

We cannot tell anything about the character of an ancestor by looking through their data of where and when they were born, married and died. To build a picture, we must begin to look at sources outside of records such as birth certificates, census returns and parish registers. One of the most useful sources to discover more about who our ancestors truly were, and in my own opinion the best source, are newspapers.

We are naturally curious to find out what the newspapers can tell us about those within our family tree. It is common for family historians, however, to give up all too easily with their search. Many believe that simply typing in their ancestor's name into an online search box will bring up all the relevant results. This is, unfortunately, untrue. When we do find our ancestor named in an article, we may not understand what it is telling us.

This book was created with all family historians in mind. You may have never searched newspapers for information before and are interested to see what you can find, or you may have used newspapers for several years but want to know how to get more out of them. You may have a selection of newspaper cuttings that have been handed down to you in your own personal family ephemera, or you may have none. Whatever your situation, this book will help you.

The history of British newspapers is discussed first to give an overview as to how the press developed. This can help you understand what information you are likely to find for each period. The chapters that follow will look at different subjects that you may find regarding your forebears in newspapers, including the criminal courts, military news and sport columns. Following these chapters, we will look at how to use newspapers as a genealogical source, including how and where to find them and issues to be aware of, such as bias and reliability. Lastly, there is a chapter on using newspapers published outside of Britain, which will be relevant if your ancestors travelled overseas.

It is my passion to help people learn more about their ancestry. Newspapers are a crucial source for this, often being the only surviving record of an event such as an engagement that was called off, a coroner's inquest whose records were destroyed or a sports match write-up. Verbatim reports are frequently provided in articles, particularly from the court room, giving us a rare chance to 'hear' our ancestor's voice and their views. At times, newspapers can help us to break down a genealogical brick wall. Articles can name relatives such as parents, siblings, children and grandparents, as well as friends, colleagues and neighbours.

As well as discovering more about our ancestors' lives where they are named specifically, newspapers can also be used to provide context and perspective. Adding more detail to a person's life story can help us to understand what the world around them was like during their lifetime. This could include local news stories such as storms, or wider news stories such as medical breakthroughs. Seeing the style and presentation of a newspaper as your ancestor would have seen it is also of interest. We can see the adverts they would have seen, the style of language that was used and see how certain topics of the day were deliberated.

My top tip for newspaper research is to never give up. Even after years of researching, I am still finding new articles about my direct line ancestors. This is partly because new publications are being digitised each week so there are new titles to research but also because even if I live to be 100 years old I still will not have exhausted every possible search term on every possible newspaper website for all of my ancestors. There is always more to research and if you ever think you have found everything about your ancestors in the newspapers I can assure you that you have not. With that in mind, take your time with your research. Try not to rush it and take notes of what and who you have researched each day, as well as where.

I hope that this book helps you to uncover a wealth of information about your ancestors. You may discover that they were injured at work, sent a letter of complaint to the editor, appealed for help to find a lost cat, were rewarded for an act of bravery or donated money to a good cause. It is sometimes the smallest pieces of information that can help us to understand who our ancestors really were, what they went through in their lifetime and how this shaped them as people.

Chapter 1

THE HISTORY OF BRITISH NEWSPAPERS

Knowing the history and evolution of newspapers in Britain can help us understand when and where we are most likely to find our ancestors in articles and how reliable these are. If you have aristocratic ancestors you are more likely to find them in newspapers in the eighteenth century than if you only have ancestors from lower classes, for example. Individual titles often have a complicated history with two or more newspapers frequently merging together to survive. For this reason, you may discover if you are browsing a particular newspaper that the title may change. Titles may also change for other reasons, such as to appeal to a wider audience or to cover a broader geographical area. As you become more familiar with searching newspapers, you will soon be able to predict the type of detail that is provided according to the date and the format within which the information is presented.

Sixteenth century

Printed individual news sheets known as 'relations' date back to at least the early sixteenth century. The earliest surviving example of this is the 1513 publication *Hereafter Ensue the Trewe Encountre or Batayle lately Don betwene Englande and Scotlande*, a copy of which can be found at the British Library. A later nineteenth-century reprint of this can be viewed online at the Internet Archive (**https://archive.org**). This is a description of the Battle of Flodden in which several knights are named; military encounters being a typical topic of the time. Also of note in England was *The Articles or Requestes of the Devonshyre and Cornyshe Rebelles* in 1549. A copy of this is held at Lambeth Palace Library. Publications of this time containing news were produced on an ad-hoc basis according to the events of the period. They were not published regularly and titles changed from one news sheet to the next, according to the topic.

Each news sheet tends to focus on one particular topic. As well as military updates, monarchs' speeches and freak weather events were also used as themes, including floods and earthquakes. In 1586, a decree from the Star Chamber required news publications to be licensed in order to avoid articles that were disloyal to the government. While news about foreign politics was allowed to be published, any political news or opinions from Britain were to be avoided.

Seventeenth century

It was not until the seventeenth century that publications appeared that we can refer to today as true newspapers. These were titled publications which were published at regular intervals. England's first titled newspaper was the *Corante*, published in London in 1621. This contained a range of European news and the earliest surviving copy is held at the British Library.

As has been frequently seen in the past, uprisings and war frequently led to a quicker rate in technological and sociological development. The English Civil War of 1642–1651 led to a greater desire by the public to read about what was happening in the country. There also appears to have been an aspiration to create propaganda to sway public opinion using publications. As a result, various newspapers began to appear, most taking the side of either the Cavaliers (otherwise known as Royalists) or the Roundheads (otherwise referred to as Parliamentarians). There are estimated to have been at least 300 different newspaper titles produced during this period, although the majority were very short-lived. Most were published monthly or weekly under titles including '*Mercurius*' or '*Intelligencer*'; Mercurius referring to Mercury, the messenger of the gods in Roman mythology. The first Scottish newspaper is believed to be *Mercurius Caledonius* published 1660–1661.

The history of *The Gazette* goes back to the seventeenth century. In 1665, due to the severity of the Great Plague in London, the Royal Court was relocated to Oxford. For this reason, the newspaper was first published there under the title of *The Oxford Gazette*. It remained so until King Charles II returned to London the following year, after which the paper has been known as *The London Gazette*. Collectively, today *The Gazette* refers to *The London Gazette*, *The Edinburgh Gazette* and *The Belfast Gazette*. *The Edinburgh Gazette* was first published in 1699 whereas *The Belfast Gazette* did not appear until 1921. *The Dublin Gazette* was published from 1706–1922 when publication ceased after the partition of

Ireland. They are all official public records of the government published by The Stationery Office. They therefore have a very different purpose and appearance from other traditional newspapers but are among the most reliable sources of the time.

Whereas most seventeenth-century newsletters and newspapers have limited appeal to a genealogist, *The Gazette* has features which are more useful to a wider range of people. Notices include the names of those appointed to public office, people granted honours, soldiers given military awards and medals, commissions and promotions in the Armed Forces and changes to coats of arms. The names of individuals declared bankrupt and naturalisations are among notices which feature the lower class and can be of huge help to our genealogical research. However, early editions name very few people. Nevertheless, famed English diarist Samuel Pepys described *The Gazette* as 'full of newes'.

As you would expect, aside from *The Gazette*, most seventeenth-century newspapers have not survived. One sad loss is what is believed to be the first Welsh language newspaper which was published monthly in Shrewsbury from 1690. There are other titles which have survived and have been digitised. These include editions of London's *Post Boy* from 1695 which can be viewed at **www.gale.com**.

Eighteenth century

The next century saw drastic changes in the newspaper industry from the start. England's first daily newspaper, the *Daily Courant*, began publication in March 1702. The first attempt at a daily newspaper had been the *Post Boy* in 1695, but this had failed after just four days. Scotland's oldest daily newspaper is *The Press and Journal*, which was not established until 1748, initially under the title of *The Aberdeen's Journal*. Other early developments in this century include evening newspapers and provincial (local) publications. The *Worcester Postman* is believed to originate from 1690; however, it was in the eighteenth century that local newspapers began to grow. Other early examples include the *Post Man* of Exeter from 1704, the *York Courant* from 1715 and Plymouth's *Weekly Journal* from 1718.

Initially, local papers copied the foreign news that had been published from the London-based editions and they did not feature local news as we know it today. For example, from 1711 the *Newcastle Courant* had the subheading 'with news forreign and domestick'. This also serves as a reminder when searching newspapers for specific text to remember that spelling was not yet standardised at this time. Words including names and place names are often written rather archaically in this period and earlier. In an edition of the *Stamford Mercury* in 1714, the place names of 'Ketring', 'Peterborow' and 'Tocester' are given rather than the Kettering, Peterborough and Towcester as we know them today.

There are early cases where local names are provided, particularly in advertisements. From the very first edition of the *Newcastle Courant* on 8 August 1711 adverts were featured. One states: 'a very good House upon the Bridge, with a Shop and Room, which formerly did belong to Isabel Hotchson, is to be Sold'. Another enlightening example features in the *Norwich Mercury* on 28 January 1727. Here it is explained that a new play entitled 'The Maid's Tragedy' is to be performed by the Norwich Company of Comedians at the King's Arms Playhouse. The names of all cast members are given along with the part they are to play. Unfortunately for us, only their surnames are given, such as Mr Duckworth is to play Diphilus and Mrs Plomer is to play Dula. You are unlikely to find ancestors named this early on; however, this shows it is possible. Generally speaking, lower classes are named if they are involved in a crime or a particularly unusual situation, such as giving birth to a large number of children or living to a much older than average age.

Under the Stamp Acts of 1712 and 1725, newspapers were subject to taxes on paper and advertisements. Stamp Duty kept the size of the newspapers small, usually folded into four pages. At this time, newspapers were still not free of government control and censorship. There was great public interest in disputes between the Whigs and Tories; however, in order to report on these, newspapers had to effectively break the law. This resulted in multiple publishers being imprisoned or fined as a deterrent to others not to copy the offence. In 1763, John Wilkes MP was arrested along with forty-eight other people after he implied in his publication, *The North Briton*, that King George III had deliberately lied in his speech. The courts threw out the charges and the government then backed down with regard to the reporting of parliamentary affairs. It was not until the nineteenth century, however, that newspapers were completely free of government interference.

Strongly linked to the newspaper industry was the magazine business. Of significance to genealogists are *The Gentleman's Magazine* published monthly from 1731 to 1922 and the lesser known *Lady's Magazine* circulated between 1770 and 1847. Contributors to the former include dictionary creator Samuel Johnson, radical political author Thomas Christie and Francis Atterbury, the Dean of Westminster Abbey. Both magazines contained articles of interest to the upper-class reader, including society news, theatre updates and poetry. Of use to us as researchers are lengthy obituaries of prominent people such as military officers and clergy, and notices of births, marriages and deaths. There was also a section headed 'Domestic Occurrences' which detailed unusual deaths. For example, in *The Gentleman's Magazine* in 1794 it is reported:

> Mr Wilkes, of Moor Lane, about 12 years of age, was looking over a board at the top of a house in a court in the Old Bailey, where he was with an engraver, the board accidentally gave way, when he fell over the parapet into the court, and fractured his skull in so shocking a manner that he expired very soon afterward.

This example also serves a reminder that, historically, much text went without punctuation as we know it today. Select copies of both magazines can be viewed for free online at **www.hathitrust.org**.

The Annual Register has been published since 1758 and is a comprehensive overview of the year's events. Much information was taken from newspapers and magazines to compile the publication and reading this can be a great way of giving context to your ancestor's life. By providing an annual summary of news, *The Annual Register* is a great source to provide a sense of historical flow. This includes military updates, royal speeches, parliamentary debates, major court cases and essays on social issues.

By the end of the eighteenth century, most cities had a daily newspaper and the majority of towns had a weekly newspaper. At this time even some foreign news was censored, such as the advancement of the French Revolution in 1789–1799. Stamp Duty was again raised in 1797 in an attempt to subdue news from France reaching the British population. The cost prevented many people from purchasing a newspaper; however, there is evidence that some were circulated among the public after the original customers had finished with their copies. Many newspapers were even read aloud in public areas, such as pubs and coffee houses, so that the illiterate among the population could discover more about the news. By this time, some big names in the industry had emerged such as *The Times* from 1785, known as the *Universal Daily Register* until 1788, and *The Observer* in 1791.

Nineteenth century

By 1815, Stamp Duty was raised to a substantial 4d. However, politicians had begun to realise that newspapers could perhaps be used to serve their own interests and be used to campaign for votes. Therefore, by 1836 the duty had been reduced to 1d and it was finally abolished on

29 June 1855. The abolishment led to a great increase in the quantity of different newspaper titles, a larger sheet size and a greater number of pages in each edition.

A lower cost meant newspapers were now available to the lower classes of society. At the beginning of the century, a newspaper would have cost around half a lower-class worker's daily wage. Men were more likely than women to be able to read, particularly those in urban areas. It was towards the end of the nineteenth century that newspaper readership began to grow rapidly. This was helped by the 1870 Elementary Education Act leading to improved literacy and therefore a greater potential readership. At this time, headlines as we know them began to appear and the format and appearance of newspapers started to change. Many Sunday newspapers were also instigated from the early to mid-nineteenth century.

The technological developments in the country also helped to grow newspaper readership during this time. Newspapers could now be produced more quickly thanks to new inventions enabling printing on both sides of a piece of paper in one go and the automatic folding of news sheets. The development of the railways from the 1830s allowed newspapers to be distributed over a wider area in a shorter time and revolutionised the industry.

From the mid-nineteenth century, you are more likely to begin finding mentions of your ancestors within local newspapers. Provincial newspapers started to rely less on news from London and abroad. Local events and happenings, which your ancestors may have been involved in such as strikes, civic celebrations and local meet-ups, are detailed. You could also use newspapers to discover when electric lighting was introduced in their area, what was being shown at the local cinema or theatre and what the big crime stories of the town were at the time. The potential of using local newspapers to discover more about your ancestor's life is beyond measure.

In Scotland, *The Courier* dates back to 1801 while *The Scotsman* originated in 1817. Other Scottish newspapers to originate in the nineteenth century include the *Perthshire Advertiser* in 1828, the *Stirling Observer* in 1836 and the *Falkirk Herald* in 1845. Notable Scottish dailies include the *Glasgow Times* from 1876 and *Daily Record* from 1895. In addition to Scottish newspapers, many British newspapers have their own edition printed for Scottish readers. These include the Scottish version of *The Sun* and the *Daily Mail* as *The Scottish Sun* and the *Scottish Daily Mail* respectively.

The Welsh newspaper industry developed massively in the nineteenth century. The first newspaper published in Wales was *The Cambrian*, which was printed in Swansea on 28 January 1804. Around a quarter of the paper was initially reserved for news from London; however, the majority of the paper is relevant to Wales. This includes shipping news, letters to the editor and a births, marriages and deaths column. Poetry also featured, along with a front page full of advertisements, which was typical of the time. The first Welsh language newspaper to be published weekly was *Seren Gomer* in 1814. The first daily newspaper published in Wales was *The Cambrian Daily Leader* on 20 May 1861 at a cost of 1d. Those interested in Welsh ancestry will find the first page of this four-page newspaper to be of most interest. For example, the first edition gives details of the latest petty session where, among many other cases, pauper Elizabeth Williams, who was to be removed from Swansea to Loughor, and Gwenllian Jones, who was charged with stealing Mary Thomas's clothes in Ystalyfera, are both named.

The Manchester Guardian began circulation in 1821, changing its title to *The Guardian* in 1959 shortly before moving its base to London. *The Daily Telegraph* was launched in 1855. The *Financial Times* was established in 1888, initially as the *London Financial Guide*. The *Daily Mail* was founded by Alfred and Harold Harmsworth in 1896 and found instant success. Over the next six years, its popularity grew rapidly and it became the newspaper with the largest circulation in the world. The 1800s are often understandably referred to as the 'golden age' of the newspaper industry with popularity growing throughout the course of the century.

Twentieth century

The twentieth century saw yet more changes in the newspaper industry. The first page-wide headline is believed to have been in the *Daily Express* on 19 May 1900 addressing the Relief of Mafeking, a morale booster for the British public regarding the Boer War, the paper itself having been established earlier the same year. The *Daily Express* was also the first to feature a crossword puzzle. The *Daily Mirror* was established in November 1903 as a newspaper produced by women aiming for a female-only readership. This idea was short-lived, however, and reverted to a newspaper aimed at both sexes six months later. The *Daily Herald* commenced publishing daily in 1912 and was relaunched in 1964 as *The Sun* due to falling sales. After a wobbly start, *The Sun* found success after it changed to become a tabloid in 1969, as we still recognise it today.

It was during the First World War that photographs were more widely used in newspapers, although for obvious reasons these could not reveal much detail that might compromise the war effort. Also during the First World War some soldiers' newspapers were created, including

Balkan News published daily in Salonika (now Thessaloniki, Greece) between 1915 and 1919 and *Wipers Times* published on a more sporadic basis from 1916 to 1919 in Ypres, Belgium. The former contained military news, usually gathered from radio reports while the latter took a more humorous approach containing jokes and comedic poetry. Few copies of either survive and it is rare to find individuals named within them. Some fake newspapers were also created and dropped behind enemy lines to cause confusion.

The use of colour in newspapers evolved greatly during the twentieth century. Britain's first colour advert appeared in Glasgow's *Daily Record* in 1936. This was a full-page advert for Dewar's White Label Whisky. This was not followed up in England until the late 1950s by the *Daily Herald*. The *Daily Record* also holds the achievement for the first colour photograph in a British newspaper, which too was published in 1936. The first British newspaper to publish a coloured photograph on its front page was *The Banbury Guardian* in 1962. The first colour national daily, titled *Today*, was launched in 1986.

Newspapers struggled during the Second World War due to heavy censorship and broadsheets being restricted to four pages each. To improve morale in Britain, any military successes were greatly overstated while any setbacks were minimised or dismissed. Reports of many battles were described with great optimism. For this reason, be wary when using contemporary papers to research military history. They are useful to read what our ancestors would have read and believed at the time but wartime was not the most reliable period in newspaper history.

During the twentieth century, provincial newspapers started to report more trivial local news items, such as school awards, sports days and parking disputes. Newspaper journalists were under the pressure of time constraints for publication to fill a set number of pages, which is why at times when there is little serious news going on, we can find more trivial stories. Journalists also started to receive recognition for their articles at this point, whereas they were previously largely anonymous. This is of little use to those of us researching any ancestors working in the industry as we cannot know which articles they contributed to before this time.

National and provincial newspapers began to recognise the potential of having websites for their readers to access towards the end of the twentieth century. Some examples include the websites of *The Daily Telegraph* which went online in 1994 at **telegraph.co.uk** and *The Times* at **thetimes.co.uk** in 1996.

Twenty-first century

This century has seen a dramatic decline in the traditional newspaper readership on paper and an increase in online readership. Further newspapers developed websites, including the *Daily Mail's MailOnline* at **dailymail.co.uk** established in 2003. Many larger newspaper titles have recently started to charge readers for online subscriptions to read their news stories. Websites are not as firmly bound by space as those printed on paper meaning more trivial news stories can be printed. These articles will surely be of interest to our descendants in years to come. More space also means there are more photographs published, as well as more advertisements.

This century has seen many newspapers cease to exist. This notably includes *An Gàidheal Ùr*, a monthly newspaper published in Scottish Gaelic which ended in 2009 and the *News of the World* in 2011. The latter announced its closure following a notorious phone-hacking scandal which brought to light the complex morality of how journalists discover news to publish.

Some newspapers now only survive online, such as *The Independent* which began in 1986 and printed its last paper copy in 2016. The ever-changing world of newspaper publishing continues to evolve. We have also seen rapid development in the number of historical newspapers that have been digitised in the last decade and these have been seemingly instantly transcribed thanks to the use of OCR (optical character recognition).

Chapter 2

BIRTHS, MARRIAGES AND DEATHS

Crucial inputs for any family tree are the dates of our ancestor's birth, marriage and death. These can frequently be found in the birth, marriage and death column of a local paper, which may also give some extra detail. Local newspapers also provided lengthier reports on some occasions outside of the regular column. This means that as well as providing a date for an event, a written feature can give a true sense of an occasion. Details of a wedding ceremony were uplifting features whereas obituaries gave readers the chance to learn about the life of a recently deceased local person. If you already have the date for your ancestor's birth, marriage and death do not make the mistake of failing to search the newspapers for more. You could miss out on a real genealogical treat!

Birth, Marriages and Deaths Column

Having a life event published in your local newspaper was originally only used by the well-known and upper classes who readers would take interest in. Later, charges were introduced so that anybody could place a notice as long as they could afford to have the information printed. Gradually, the cost was reduced and the column became more accessible to our poorer ancestors. Charges varied according to each paper. *Eddowes's Shrewsbury Journal* in 1885 charged 1 shilling per birth announcement. In the same year, *The Bristol Times and Mirror* charged 1 shilling for the first sixteen words and 5 pence for every additional eight words for a placement in the column. Common abbreviations you are likely to come across are 'ult.' and 'inst.' 'Ult.' is an abbreviation for 'Ultimo' referring to the previous month. 'Inst.' is a contraction of 'instant' meaning the current month. Entries in the column may therefore refer to events that occurred in the same month that the newspaper was published, or the month prior.

A typical column gives fairly minimal information. For a birth, a date of birth is usually given along with the name of one or both parents. Initially, only the sex of the child was provided but eventually it became normal for the child's name to be stated. A representative early example from *The Lynn Advertiser and West Norfolk Herald* on 6 December 1845 states: 'On the 29th ult., at Holbeach, Mrs Edward Key, of a son'. Many eighteenth-century columns focused solely on marriages and deaths. When birth notices were introduced, some newspapers chose to publish the births of sons and the births of daughters in separate sections. Others displayed them in chronological order by date of birth, but most are presented in alphabetical order by surname. The father's occupation may be given and sometimes the mother's maiden name with a home address. A later typical example can be seen in the *Llanelli Star* on 31 December 1949 which states: 'JONES – On Christmas Day at Glasfryn to Mr and Mrs D. R. Jones (née Beryl King), 55 Bigyn Road, the gift of a son, David Christopher'.

Stillbirths were frequently reported in the births column, particularly in the nineteenth century. These appear alongside the other birth notices with the only differing detail being the word 'stillborn', usually in brackets at the end of the notice. One example can be seen in the Exeter-based paper *The Western Times* on 8 January 1878: 'CAMPBELL – Jan 5th at 17 The Mint, Exeter, the wife of Colin Campbell, of a son – stillborn'. An occasion of multiple births would also be noted as in the case of twins, triplets or much rarer cases of higher numbers. These may be found in the births column or as a separate article. Multiple births were much more likely to result in stillbirth. An example of this can be seen in the sad case on the following page where a quintuplet pregnancy resulted in the deaths of all five babies in Rothes, Moray in Scotland.

Marriage notices gave the names of the bride and groom, the date of the marriage and often the names of their fathers and place of residence. The bride or groom's placement within the family may be stated, such as: 'the eldest daughter of John Smith married the second son of Samuel Turner.' If the family was wealthy, the announcement was generally lengthier and included the name of the clergy that married the happy couple and details of the family's peerage. In these situations, a person's title may be given instead of their name, such as in December 1776 when the marriage of the Earl of Radnor to Miss Duncombe was announced in multiple papers. If you were therefore searching for their marriage

BIRTHS.

April 19, Viscountess Folkestone, of twins—a son and a daughter.

April 19, the Countess of Arran, of a daughter.

At London, Agril 19, the Hon. Mrs Wm. Napier, of a daughter.

At the house of her father, Sir H. Ferguson Davie, Bart., M.P., Wilton Crescent, London, April 22, the wife of Major Thomson, King's Dragoon Guards, of a son.

At 15 Chester Street, Kennington, London, April 16, a poor woman, the wife of a journeyman printer, of three fine male children, who, as well as the mother, are progressing favourably.

Five Children at One Birth !—On the morning of Monday week, a woman of the name of Elspet Gordon, residing in Rothes, gave birth to three male and two female children. The three boys were born alive and lived till the following morning, but the two girls were still-born. The births were premature, being in the sixth month ; but what was very extraordinary, all were full grown for the period of gestation ; nor is this the most surprising circumstance in the case, one of the boys having actnally two front teeth when he came into the world. Dr Dawson, Rothes, attended the woman, who we are happy to say, is doing wonderfully well.—*Elgin Courant.*

Births column from *The Montrose Arbroath & Brechin Review* dated 30 April 1858 showing three separate cases of multiple births. *(Content provided by the British Library Board. All rights reserved. With thanks to The British Newspaper Archive (www.britishnewspaperarchive.co.uk))*

in the column using their names of Jacob Pleydell-Bouverie and Anne Duncombe you would not see the results. Notices from the eighteenth century sometimes give an estimate of the bride's dowry or 'portion'.

Marriages of the lower classes can be more commonly found from the 1880s onwards. A typical marriage notice would appear similar to this example in the *South Eastern Gazette* on 15 June 1915: 'MILLEN – COLLS – June 10th at Holy Trinity Church, Sittingbourne, by the Rev. J.C. Eyre Kidson, Vicar, Leonard, fourth son of Mr Alfred Millen, of Sittingbourne, to Marguerite Mary, twin daughter of Mr William Colls, of Peterborough'. As with all notices, information was often kept short, as the person placing it was charged by the line or by the word.

For death announcements, the deceased's name, age and date of death is given often with their parish of residence. Extra information may include a person's occupation, a cause of death and a specific home address. The name of the deceased's spouse may also be given. A respected housekeeper or servant's death may be noted by their employer. By the beginning of the twentieth century, it is more likely that

MARRIAGE.

By ſpecial licence, the Hon. Mr. Bingham, eldeſt ſon of Lord Lucan, to Lady Elizabeth Howard.

DEATHS.

At Madrid, in the 21ſt year of his age, the Duke of Berwick, ſon to the Princeſs of Sangro, and laſt male iſſue of Marſhal Berwick, natural ſon to James II. of England. ---In Chelſea Hoſpital, Joſhua Crewman, a Chelſea penſioner, aged 123 years. He ſerved in the reign of George I. and II. and was diſcharged in the 74th year of his age.

Marriages and deaths seen on the front page of the *Hereford Journal* on 4 June 1794. *(With permission from Midland News Association)*

some additional personal information may be supplied, such as 'after much suffering', 'suddenly' or 'after a short illness'. The date and location of the deceased's upcoming funeral may also be given. A representative example of a death entry is seen in the *Bucks Herald* on 12 February 1859 stating: 'SEDGWICK – On the 5th inst., at 5 Westbourne Park, London, Elizabeth, widow of the late Mr John Sedgwick, of Rickmansworth, Herts'. The image above and on the following page are examples from a birth, marriage and death column that are typical of their time.

Some newspapers presented life event information in a different format. London-based newspaper *The Weekly Chronicle* was known to publish information in lengthy paragraphs. Surnames were not capitalised and can be easily missed. Other titles grouped deaths together by location, with the town of residence in bold followed by the names and ages of the dead.

You can find other genealogical details in a births, marriages and deaths column that may surprise you. Names of grandparents are sometimes given, such as if a bride's grandfather was a notable figure or if the deceased died at the home of their grandparent or grandchild. Historically, some newspapers included notices of bankruptcy in the

BIRTHS, MARRIAGES, DEATHS.

BIRTHS.

NEWBY—On 26th July, at Portchester, to Lieut. and Mrs. E. J. Newby, a son.

MARRIAGES.

BROWN—ABEL—On 29th July, at Bromley, Kent, Eng.-Capt. P. R. T. Brown, R.N., to Kate R. Abel (Kitty), elder daughter of the late Mr. and Mrs. James Abel, of Shortlands Kent.

McCONNELL—BINDING—On August 2nd, at the Registry Office, by special licence, the second son of the late Mr. and Mrs. McConnell, of Norwich, to Dorothy Kate Binding, third daughter of George Binding of Eastney.

DEATHS.

JUSTICE—In loving memory of John Archibald Justice, age 25 years, late 1-6th Hants Regt., who passed away 31st July, 1922, after a short illness.—From his loving mother, father, brothers and sisters.

LUSH—On August 1st, at 13, Sussex-road, Southsea, Isaac Edgcumbe Lush. No mourning or flowers by special request.

The births, marriages and deaths column from *The Hampshire Telegraph* dated 4 August 1922. *(Content provided by the British Library Board. All rights reserved. With thanks to The British Newspaper Archive (www.britishnewspaperarchive.co.uk))*

column which today looks very out of place. One such example can be seen in the *Ipswich Journal* on 17 August 1751 when draper Benjamin Greene of Ampthill in Bedfordshire was declared bankrupt.

Over time, the births, marriages and deaths column evolved to include more life events such as adoptions, christenings, engagements, wedding anniversaries, notable birthdays and in memoriam notices. Messages of thanks and congratulations can also be seen. During the two world wars, Rolls of Honour could be seen alongside the deaths column naming recently deceased soldiers and their regiment. It became custom in some American newspapers in the mid- to late nineteenth century to have columns

> **B I R T H.**
> The Lady of the Hon. Admiral Boscawen, delivered of a Son, at his House in South Audley-Street
> **B A N K R U P T.**
> Benjamin Greene, of Ampthill, Bedfordshire, Draper.
> **M A R R I A G E.**
> Sir William Maynard, Bart. to Miss Charlotta Bishop, second Daughter of Sir Cecil Bishop, Bart.
> **D E A T H.**
> Dr. Thomas Crowe, of Throgmorton Street, one of the Vice-Presidents of St. Luke's Hospital for Lunaticks.

An example of a births, bankrupts, marriages and deaths column from *The Ipswich Journal* dated 17 August 1751. (*Content provided by the British Library Board. All rights reserved. With thanks to The British Newspaper Archive (www.britishnewspaperarchive.co.uk)*)

headed 'Marriages, Divorces and Deaths'; however, the reporting of divorces in the births, marriages and deaths column never took off in Britain. Where engagements are reported, this does not necessarily mean that a marriage took place as was intended. There are even some marriage notices in newspapers which were never formally registered as a legal marriage.

The columns in Welsh newspapers can give further genealogical information due to the patronymic naming traditions in Wales. The surname of the child usually refers to the father's first name. There are exceptions, and full-blood brothers can end up having different surnames. The names help to preserve the ancestral names of the male line, such as 'Gwilym ap Sion ap Ellis ap Owain'. Ap or ab means 'son of', so this would translate into William son of John son of Ellis son of Owen. There are cases where up to six generations of family names have been provided, usually in the deaths section.

Many Nonconformist denominations ran their own newspapers, which also carried birth, marriage and death columns. An appearance here may be the first time you come across evidence that your ancestor was a Nonconformist. This can then be used to trace them in related records of their chosen denomination. The appearance and information supplied in the column is very much the same as in a non-secular newspaper column and, as with other newspapers, a charge was applied to those wishing to place a notice. Examples can be seen in the *Methodist Times*, *The Nonconformist and Independent* and *The Catholic Times and Catholic Opinion*.

The column can be of most use prior to July 1837 when civil registration was introduced. Before this time, official certificates for birth, marriages and deaths do not exist, so a mention in a column may be the only source providing a date of birth, marriage or death for a person. The column is also useful where the correct certificate cannot be found. Notices may also provide more information than is supplied on a certificate. Therefore, even when a certificate has been purchased, it is still worth searching the newspapers in case extra information has been reported.

Newspaper editors usually requested proof of the event prior to publication, particularly after 1837, meaning the reliability of the births, marriages and deaths column tends to be greater than other sections of a newspaper. As well as finding events given in the newspaper local to the area in which it occurred, it may also be published in others where relevant. A wealthy landowner from Aberdeen who married in Ayr may have his marriage published in both areas, for example. Notable people may also have their events published in national as well as local newspapers.

In Memoriam

Usually included in the births, marriage and deaths column, the 'in memoriam' notice section was a later addition. They tend to be seen from the latter half of the nineteenth century onwards. For the newspapers it was an additional way of creating revenue, and for loved ones it was a way of remembering their departed family member or friend. In memoriam notices peaked in popularity in the twentieth century; however, they are still frequently seen in local papers today. The information supplied depends entirely on the person who placed the notice. Most consist of a few short lines noting the name of the deceased, the date they died and the name of the person who placed the notice. Many are written in the first person giving us a chance to read our ancestors' own words.

The same, or similar, notices were often posted annually by loved ones. This may be on the anniversary of the deceased's death or on another notable date such as their birthday. An example is in the *Somerset Guardian* on 13 October 1933: 'DANDO – In loving memory of a dear wife and mother, Mary Ann Dando, who passed away at Timsbury, on Oct. 12th 1930. Ever remembered by husband and family'. The family of Mary Ann Dando posted an in memoriam notice annually for many years after her death.

Other in memoriam notices were much longer and some even pass as a short obituary. A cause of death is sometimes given, particularly if the deceased was a soldier who died in action. The notice may mention if a person is 'presumed dead' after being reported missing for a long time. Others contain poems of several verses or excerpts from religious texts. The information supplied is interesting to read in itself, but it also shines a light onto the relationship that the notice's author had with the deceased. Many give a true heartfelt insight into the devastating grief suffered by spouses, parents and children.

Marriages

Reports of wedding ceremonies can commonly be found outside of the births, marriages and deaths column under a heading of their own. As with similar reports, they initially focused on the upper classes, but by the early twentieth century you may find these for an ancestor from any background. The first separate marriage reports tend to relate to royalty and appear in national and local newspapers. In the *Chester Chronicle* on 26 May 1797 the wedding of Charlotte, Princess Royal, to the then Prince of Württemberg is described in great detail, especially their attire. This includes the dresses of the bride, Queen Charlotte and the bridesmaids with a small description of the groom and King George III's outfit.

In the early nineteenth century, marriage reports still focused on the upper classes. The detail was usually limited and focused on informing readers of the bride's and groom's ancestry, such as if their fathers were peers or military officers. Any extravagant elements to the ceremony were noted, such as in the *Morning Post* on 11 August 1821 where Lady Mary Poulet is said to have worn a 'very costly dress composed of Valenciennes lace' when she wed Lord Charles Somerset. They left for their honeymoon in a chariot pulled by four horses.

From the 1840s onwards, marriage reports boomed. It is thought this may have been due to the popular matrimony of Queen Victoria and Prince Albert in 1840. Every decade afterwards sees a sharp increase in the number of marriages having their own separate reports in newspapers outside of the usual column entry. Despite their popularity, the majority of people would not have had their marriages reported on in this way. You are most likely to find a marriage report relevant to your family in the first half of the twentieth century.

These short articles would typically give the names of the bride and groom and either one or both of their parents' names. Their occupations may be given if they are notable. The date and location of their marriage will be given, sometimes with the time of the ceremony. Names of the wedding party are frequently given and in some cases the name of everybody who attended and their relationship to the bride or groom. Descriptions of their attire may be given along with the flowers and hymns that were chosen. Presents given to the couple may be listed. In some lucky examples, you may find a photograph of the bride and

WEDDINGS.

MANN — SINCLAIR.

A pretty wedding took place on Tuesday, at Old St. Pancras Church, the contracting parties being the daughter of Mr William Sinclair with Mr Edgar Montague Mann. The bride's father has been for many years a respected member of the St. Pancras Iron Works, having served his time under the present member for East St. Pancras, Sir Thomas Wrightson, and since his residence in the district he has worked hard for the Conservative cause. Mr Mann is the son of Mr E. M. Mann, journalist, of Bridgnorth, near Exeter. As it was only a few yards' walk from the bride's father's address to the church there were no carriages, and the neighbours all said they had never seen a livelier or brighter wedding, the genial father leading the bride, followed by the bridesmaids, the Misses Emily Taylor, Edith Mann, Fanny Rogers, and Kathleen Sinclair, escorted by the best man Mr Arthur H. Mann, and by Mr John B. Mann and a large contingent of fellow employés from the Railway Clearing House. The presents were very numerous. The honeymoon is being spent at Torquay.

A wedding report from *St. Pancras Gazette* 13 April 1901 detailing the Mann/Sinclair nuptials. Note that the bride is not named so this image would not turn up in results if you searched using her name. *(Content provided by the British Library Board. All rights reserved. With thanks to The British Newspaper Archive (www.britishnewspaperarchive.co.uk))*

groom, sometimes with family members also present. The article often ends with the location of the couple's forthcoming honeymoon.

Some marriage reports had their own headings. Others can be found under the local news. My maternal grandparents' wedding was noted under the title of 'Bletchley' in the *Bedfordshire Times* on 13 February 1942.

This is a short report similar to what would be found in the marriages column. Conversely, my paternal grandparents' marriage report appears under the heading of 'Bank Holiday Wedding' in the *Western Gazette* on 11 August 1939. This details my grandmother's dress, flowers and the hymns that were sung. The best man and bridesmaid are named, both of whom were relations. The image on the previous page is an example of what you may find. In this case, more details are supplied about the fathers of the bride and groom than they themselves.

Funeral Reports

The date and location of a person's funeral was often noted in the 'Deaths' column of their local newspaper. For some people, this was followed at a later date by a funeral report. These are more commonly found from the latter half of the nineteenth century. This was a separate article placed in the newspapers giving details of the proceedings and can tell us where our ancestor was buried. These reports were again initially only for the upper classes and those well known in their community before spreading through the lower classes.

Funeral reports usually begin with a brief obituary of the deceased, giving their name, age at death and marital status. Their place of residence and place of death are normally provided. The date and location of the funeral is given, followed by the name of the clergy who presided. At the end of the report, the names of the funeral attendees are given, described as 'mourners'. There is often a separate list of names of those who provided floral tributes. These names may be different if somebody could not attend but wished to send a tribute. The list of mourners may be quite basic, such as 'Mr Smith, Mrs Smith, Mr Jones, Mrs Jones ...' or it may go into great detail giving the full names of those who attended and their relationship to the deceased. The latter is obviously of a much greater use to a family historian. In some sad cases, it is noted that there were no family mourners present. As well as familial relationships, other attendees are described as colleagues, employees, friends and neighbours giving you a new avenue to research. The names of businesses, clubs and other organisations with which the deceased was associated may also be given.

In lengthier funeral reports, details of the service are given, including hymns that were sung, religious readings that were chosen and a description of the coffin. In some later cases, from the twentieth century onwards, a photograph of the deceased is provided. Pall bearers may be named, the breastplate text transcribed and the flower arrangements may be described. It is sometimes noted what flowers were dropped into the grave during the burial. For example, in the *Staffordshire Sentinel* on 24 November 1926, it is noted that at the funeral of William Edward Challinor, members of the St Edwards Lodge of Freemasons placed sprigs of acacia onto the coffin. At many soldiers' funerals, poppies were dropped into the grave.

Obituaries

An obituary is the notification of a person's death along with their brief life story. The information in an obituary can be very useful to a genealogist with information about the deceased's birth, parents, siblings, places of residence and occupations among other details. The more modern obituaries will probably carry a photograph of the deceased. As researchers, we need to be aware that the information in an obituary may not be entirely reliable. Details were generally given by the deceased's loved ones, such as their spouse and children, and they may not have provided the most accurate detail. Just as an age can be inaccurate on a death certificate, so it can in an obituary. Similarly, where a place of birth is so often incorrect on a census return so it may be in an obituary. Historically, people were less concerned with knowing their accurate place and date of birth. Many people assumed that they were born in the first place they could remember residing in their living memory and were unaware that their parents had relocated since their birth. It is important to bear this in mind when trying to track down an ancestor's birth certificate or baptism register entry.

Lengthy obituaries can be seen in journals and national newspapers, such as *Gentleman's Magazine* which particularly focused on clergymen and military officers. Regimental journals published obituaries for deceased officers. Obituaries for the very wealthy can be found in the eighteenth century, but you are far more likely to find one from the nineteenth century onwards. They tend to relate to people of note. Apart from royalty, peers and wealthy businessmen, you may also discover an obituary published for an ancestor who died of very old age, usually over the age of 90. My fourth great-grandmother Eleanor Marshall of Longdon, Staffordshire had her obituary published in the *Lichfield Mercury* after she died at the age of 94 on 5 January 1900. The name and occupation of her father is given along with the details of her second husband and how many of their children had outlived her. Eleanor is stated to have been known locally as 'Granny Marshall' who was a 'true lover of the country' and 'frequently took long walks in the fields'. While it sounds like Eleanor lived a full life, it was otherwise unassuming and had she not lived so long the obituary would not have been published and these details would have been lost. Obituaries are a less common find for our lower-class ancestors. Another reason you may discover one for a poorer ancestor is if they were known for committing a crime, particularly if the crime had led to their execution.

Back to the first point about being wary of the accuracy of obituaries – spare a thought for the editor of the *Chester Chronicle*. On 22 July 1791, the newspaper was forced to print a correction regarding the obituary published the previous week relating to actress Miss M. Hamilton after it discovered she was actually still alive! This is a very good example as to why finding corroborating sources is so important in genealogical research.

Bills of Mortality

Bills of mortality were statistics published weekly, monthly or annually regarding the number of births and deaths in London and the outskirts of the capital. Commonly, causes of death are also given and often deaths are further categorised according to the age of death. The initial aim of keeping such statistics was so that officials could keep an eye out for any plague outbreaks and research any potential spreading of disease in an area. You can find bills of mortality in many national and local newspapers. While they will not name an ancestor, it can give you an idea of what causes of death were rife at the time of their decease.

You will find that historically causes of death were very different, especially for the statistics in the eighteenth century. Deaths caused by dental issues were often high due to a lack of education with regard to dental care and the treatment of infections. Deaths during childbirth for both mother and baby were also much higher for similar reasons. Many of the medical terms used are now obsolete, such as 'tissick' for tuberculosis and 'rising of the lights' referring to lung conditions. If you are aware of the cause of death of your ancestor from another source, it can be interesting to see how many others died locally of the same cause at that time. The statistics were often published in local newspapers in counties far away from London due to a general public health interest. The example on the following page from the *Stamford Mercury* on 25 October 1716 gives a good example of what you can discover. You will note that many medical terms are out of date and other causes of death are vague, such as 'aged' and 'suddenly'.

From 11 January 1840, the bills of mortality were replaced by the weekly returns of the Registrar General. Updates can still be found in newspapers under the heading of bills of mortality. This may seem confusing; however, the information was gathered for the same reasons and can be used by researchers in the same way.

At times of disease outbreaks, more column space was given to bills of mortality to focus on updating readers on growing epidemics. One example is the cholera outbreak of 1848–1849. At such times, extra details

London, Octob. 18.
Bills of Mortality, from Octob. 9. to Oct. 16.

Aged	36	Fever	36	Spotted Fever	2
Apoplexy	1	Fistula	1	Stilborn	11
Asthma	1	French-Pox	1	Stone	1
Bloody-Flux	1	Gravel	1	Stoppage in Stomach	4
Cancer	1	Griping in the Guts	7	Strongullion	1
Childbed	5	Imposthume	1	Suddenly	4
Chrisoms	2	Measles	10	Teeth	25
Colick	2	Mortification	1	Thrush	1
Consumption	44	Rickets	1	Tissick	30
Convulsion	102	Rising of the Lights	1	Worms	1
Dropsie	36	Small-Pox	124		

C A S U A L T I E S.

Bruised by a Fall from the Fore-yard of a Ship at St. John Wapping 1. Executed 8. Kill'd accidentally 2. One by a Fall out of a Window at St Giles without Cripplegate, and One by a Fall from a Horse at Wapping. Overlaid 1.

Christened ———— 360
Buried ———— 454.
Decreased in the Burials this Week 20.

Bills of Mortality from *Stamford Mercury* on 25 October 1716. Note that causes of death by accident are given in more detail underneath the more common reasons. *(Content provided by the British Library Board. All rights reserved. With thanks to The British Newspaper Archive (www.britishnewspaperarchive.co.uk))*

were often supplied which may be of use to researchers. For example, in London's *The Patriot* on 2 November 1848 under a headline of 'The Cholera' the weekly death statistics for the capital are given. These include other causes of death initially, such as 166 from tuberculosis and 51 due to pneumonia. The details of those who died from cholera are then given in extra detail such as:

Spinster, 30 years, 6 Baker Street, North Brixton, 'cholera Asiatica (36 hours' duration)'. She worked in a garden. Widow, 34 years, 6 Baker Street, North Brixton, 'malignant Asiatic cholera (16 hours' duration)'. Spinster in Peckham-house Lunatic Asylum, 18 years, 'spasmodic cholera (54 hours' duration)'.

It is easy to spot that the first two victims were residing in the same property. The information at this time was gathered from the Registrar General and contains the same information as you would find on their death certificate. As you can see in the above example, a search using a London-based ancestor's name would not bring up a positive search result, meaning you would need to search for the death statistics for that week and their address.

Chapter 3

ACCIDENTS AND NATURAL DISASTERS

Researching ancestors who were involved in an accident or a natural disaster involve similar techniques. This is because they can either occur on a small scale such as localised flooding or a fall from height, or on a much larger scale such as a wildfire or a mining disaster. Those that occurred on a small scale are much more likely to name your ancestor and give identifiable details such as their age and address. If your ancestor was involved in a disaster of any kind they may not be named at all.

If you are already aware from oral history or other sources that your ancestor was involved in an incident this can make it easier to track down articles about the event. Searching for your ancestor by name will not always bring up a result in these cases, but if you know that they were involved in a workplace accident in a certain factory in a known year this gives you some great search terms to use to bring up relevant results.

If you are not sure if your ancestor was involved in an incident of these types, the first port of call should be as always to search by their name and all variations of it on a newspaper database. This may bring up results. If not, the next step should be to search using their place of residence, narrowing the results down to the time you know that they lived there. If the place was a small village or hamlet this can be really useful at discovering notable local events, particularly if you narrow results down using an extra search term such as 'disaster', 'flooding' or 'fire'.

It will be useful to you to research the local history of your ancestor's residences. Any large events that occurred there may already have been researched and possibly some of the smaller ones too. You can choose to do this by reading local history books or by using a search engine to see what turns up. Once you find that an incident has occurred, you can then use this to filter results down on a newspaper database online.

Major events will have multiple articles spread across numerous local and national newspapers over many days. The largest events will be discussed over several years, even decades later. Today we still see newspaper reports on the 1912 sinking of *Titanic* looking at new evidence for example. Smaller events may only feature in one short piece in a local newspaper. Even these may have follow-up details, however, such as if an injured person later died or new evidence came to light. Expand the years of your search as you progress through your research. Looking at multiple publications will also help you to avoid potential bias, especially if journalists wished to pin the blame of an industrial accident on a particular party.

There are likely to be some overlaps with this chapter and other related ones. For example, if an accident resulted in a death there may be reports of a coroner's inquest in the local newspaper, details of which can be read in the following chapter 'Criminal and Court Reports'. Their death may also feature in the local births, marriages and deaths column, perhaps with an obituary following. As always, ensure you have exhausted all possible search terms relating to an incident involving your ancestor. Missing an article could result in losing an important piece of information.

Discovering a natural disaster or large-scale accident that occurred within the parish your ancestor was residing is an important fact to add to their timeline. Even if they were not seemingly involved in any way, it would most probably have impacted their lives. Put yourself in their shoes to think about how such an incident may have affected them. You may find a lightning strike brought down power lines which may have left them without electricity for a number of days; a flood that damaged their local church; or an accident at their workplace meaning their factory had to be shut down.

Accidents and Incidents

Accidents can occur anywhere. They are most likely to feature in a newspaper if they caused severe injuries or death and if they occurred in the workplace or in public. Minor accidents within the home rarely feature, unless there is something unusual about the occurrence, such as a well-known public figure being involved. Journalists often spoke to witnesses of an accident to give a first-hand account of the story, although not all were willing to talk.

Where verbatim accounts are given, we should remember the potential issues surrounding the reliability of their statements. A witness to a car crash may be suffering from shock and not remember things clearly. If the witness knew who was at fault but did not want to draw attention to this then they may lie about what they saw. Generally speaking, the longer the period of time that has passed after an event the more likely falsehoods will creep in, so check the date of the article against the date of the accident itself.

As well as researching ancestors who have been injured or witnessed an injury, we may also have an ancestor who was accused of causing an accident. This again may appear in an update about the event or in a resulting inquiry or inquest. Finding out the result of the case will be an important part of their story.

I have written in a later chapter about my great great-grandfather Alexander Taylor (1865–1920) as he was a prolific criminal in Maidstone, Kent. His death certificate states that he died from a head injury after a fall from a lorry in Allington. It was noted, as you would expect, that his death was investigated by the coroner, however, as you would again expect, the inquest details have not survived. At the time of receiving Alexander's death certificate, a search of newspaper databases brought up no results. This was the same whether I searched for his exact name, variations such as Alex and 'Alexr' as it is sometimes shortened to, spelling errors such as Tyler instead of Taylor and searching for terms such as 'lorry' and 'Allington'. The inquest simply did not appear.

I somewhat naturally assumed that Alexander had died during a criminal act, perhaps stealing goods from the back of the lorry or acting drunk and disorderly as he so often did. Luckily, a newspaper article was uploaded in 2021, many years after my initial search, which proved me wrong. His name has not been transcribed correctly by OCR, appearing in the search results as 'Akaander Taylor', showing how wrong words can often be translated. To discover a result, I searched by his surname and narrowed the results down to the month of his death and the county of Kent.

In the *Kent Messenger & Maidstone Telegraph* on 14 August 1920, the details of the accident that resulted in Alexander's death are described. Alexander had received a lift in a lorry with some fellow colleagues travelling from Aylesford to Maidstone after finishing work and had climbed onto the top canopy above the driver's seat. After hitting a bump in the road Alexander had fallen off the lorry into the road and fractured his skull. This article gives me a huge range of information about Alexander that is not available elsewhere. His wife, Alice, my great

Maidstone Labourer Killed.

Having obtained a " lift" in a motor lorry from Preston Hall, Aylesford, into Maidstone on Monday evening, Alexander Taylor, aged 56, of 22, Market Street, Maidstone, climbed on to the canopy over the driver's seat, but shortly after was thrown off, and death ensued the same evening from a fracture of the base of the skull.

The inquest was held at the West Kent General Hospital on Thursday by the Borough Coroner, Mr. W. H. Day. Mr. R. Brennan represented Messrs. Wallis and Co., Ltd., the lorry driver, and the Insurance Company.

Mrs. Taylor, the widow, who lives at 23, Western Road, said her husband was a builder's labourer employed by Messrs. Wallis. They had not lived together for ten years.

George Horton, 11, Whitehall Place, employed by Messrs. Wallis and Sons, said on Monday he was working at Preston Hall with deceased. They left at 5 o'clock and came along the London Road on the firm's lorry. Witness was sitting with the driver, and when they got to the Railway Arch he felt a sudden bump and was pitched up against the left-hand side of the seat. At that moment he saw deceased fall from the back of the lorry. He thought deceased was inside the lorry. The driver pulled up and deceased was moved to the bank. Witness was not talking to the driver, who had both hands on the wheel.

Extract from *The Kent Messenger & Maidstone Telegraph* on 14 August 1920 describing the accident which resulted in the death of my second great-grandfather Alexander Taylor. *(With permission from KM Group)*

great-grandmother, stated she and Alexander had not lived together for ten years. This explains why she remarried just a few weeks after Alexander's death, as she had clearly already moved on. His time of death is given as 11.20 p.m. and his nickname of 'Pouchy' is given. The last words he heard before his fall were stated to be, 'Don't sit up there

Pouchy, the branches will knock you off,' after which he moved position inwards.

As well as accidents that resulted in deaths, articles about more minor incidents can be of interest. You may find an agricultural labourer who was kicked by a horse, a driver who fell off their cart or a child who fell into an icy lake. Sometimes by finding out about these earlier injuries it can help to make sense of their later ailments, such as if they walked with a limp or had a crooked nose where it was once broken.

Any accident report may provide genealogical information, no matter how minor the injury or property damage. In *The Dorset County Express* on 30 November 1869, a report regarding a 6-year-old boy who fell off a donkey at Preston and fractured his arm provides the name of his father as Charles Miller, a gardener, and his grandfather, who was with the boy at the time, as John Miller. The boy himself is not named but would be easy enough for a researcher to work out with the given information. The report also quotes that Dr Rhodes of Weymouth attended the scene, highlighting the fact that any ancestors who worked in the medical field or other branches of emergency services may also be named in accident reports.

There are of course major incidents that will be reported in local and national newspapers over several running issues. Examples include the 1930 Glen Cinema disaster, the 1918 mining disaster at Minnie Pit and the 1936 fire at Crystal Palace. Any accident resulting in multiple deaths, the loss of a famous building or landmark or the death of a well-known person will feature a great deal in newspapers. For these large-scale events, it is essential to recognise the importance of using a variety of sources. Authors of books on the subject will have researched the topic thoroughly, so while it is important to read the newspapers' contemporary account, it is also crucial to read around the subject. The same goes for major natural disasters.

As an example of how large-scale incidents are reported, we can look at the Blantyre mining disaster of 1877, when at least 207 people died. An explosion occurred within the pits at 9:30 a.m. on 22 October. Reports of the incident appeared in newspapers on the same day in a variety of evening publications. These include the *Birmingham Daily Mail*, *Edinburgh Evening News* and the *Evening Express* of Liverpool. The news had reached journalists via telegram and initial reports were vague with factual errors, as you would expect. Despite this being a huge story, the news does not appear on the front page at this time.

In the first report in the *Edinburgh Evening News* on 22 October 1877, the scene of the accident is described, including how women and children were crowding around the pit opening in a scene that is 'most harrowing'. Even on this same-day report, four of the deceased are named. The *Birmingham Daily Mail* on the same day overestimated the number of people who had died stating: 'it is feared that the whole of the 400 men entombed in Mr Dixon's pit, Blantyre, Glasgow, have perished.' At the time of the report, twenty bodies had been recovered, but none were named in this issue.

The following day, the number of reports on the incident increases dramatically, as you would expect. The daily morning newspapers had additional time to gather further information, although this was a story that was to develop over several weeks with the recovery of further bodies and later inquiries. Men who had been rescued alive, as well as those who had died, are named, along with those helping with the rescue effort. The manager, Mr Watson, named as being at the pit head, was badly burnt himself. After twenty-four hours, knocking was still being heard, giving hope to loved ones that further people might be rescued. The crowds are described as growing. As the story involved so many deaths, it was reported in almost every national and local newspaper in Britain.

The aftermath features in hundreds of newspaper articles. The recovery efforts continued for several weeks, with names of inspectors given as well as the names of the deceased as they were confirmed. By 10 November 1877, the *Paisley & Renfrewshire Gazette* estimated there were still seventy-one men unaccounted for. This article also names those who have been helping those affected by the tragedy in their own charitable way, such as Lady Emily Hamilton who supplied ninety mourning dresses for the widows and Mrs Dixon who donated £100 for the provision of clothes and blankets for those in need. There are reports on many of the men's funerals, as well as how they were identified. In the same article mentioned above, it is noted that 20-year-old Thomas Roberts was identified by his mother thanks to his sock that she had recently repaired.

Men listed as deceased or unidentified were regularly listed in newspapers. The lists often contain details of interest, including some genealogically relevant detail. In *The Glasgow Herald* on 31 October 1877, it is stated one of the dead was 'Archibald M'Killop, 13, drawer, residing in Windsor Street, Burnbank. Identified by his father, John M'Killop, who has a son still in the mine.' One of the unidentified men is described as being a young man with several nails in his vest pocket, with a belt and a flask.

An official inquiry began on 12 November 1877. The senior figures who attended are named and verbatim reports are supplied in multiple

June 18, 1764.

WHereas a sudden Fire happened at Rowton, in the Parish of High-Arcall, Shropshire, on the 28th of May last past, whereby Seven Farm Houses, with all their Out-buildings, and two Cottages, were burnt down in a surprizing short Time, so that little of any Account of their Goods, Implements of Husbandry, or even Wearing Apparel could be saved, to the great Damage of the poor Sufferers, whose Loss, upon a careful Estimate, amounts to Nine Hundred Pounds and upwards: The Sufferers are advised not to Petition Charity in their own Persons; but a Collection for their Use will be made by Gentlemen, and Persons of Character, who will be personally known to those they solicit: Therefore if any Persons, not answering the above Description, shall be found asking Charity on Account of the said Fire they may be taken up for Impostors.

N. B. Any well disposed Persons desirous of contributing to this Charity, may send such Contribution to Charles Bolas, Esq; of Shrewsbury.

A report in *Aris's Birmingham Gazette* dated 25 June 1764 detailing a fire within High Ercall and giving information regarding donations to those affected. *(With permission from Archives and Collections, Birmingham Libraries)*

newspaper titles. The reports on the inquiry give a clear picture of the events that happened that day and the days following. Many of the miners are named, whether they survived or died. They are essential reading for anybody whose ancestor was involved in any way with the Blantyre mining disaster.

As an example of how difficult it can be to trace relevant incidents, the extract in the image above details a fire that occurred in High Ercall, Shropshire. The report from *Aris's Birmingham Gazette* dates from 25 June 1764 and describes how a fire quickly spread throughout nine properties and several outbuildings. This example demonstrates why you may find it difficult to get a positive result from an online search. Due to the date of the article, the long 's' is used for a lower-case 's' which is usually transcribed by OCR as an 'f' so words are interpreted differently, such as 'Shropfhire' for Shropshire. No names are given of those affected by the fire so a name search will give no results. The name of the parish is also written as 'High-Arcall' so even a parish search will have no results.

Natural Disasters

You may be aware from an historical source that your ancestor's life was impacted by a natural disaster, such as a flood, earthquake or storm. This could be through oral history, a diary or photographs of the aftermath.

If you already have this knowledge, you can use what you know to find relevant local newspaper articles about the event. First try searching online using the terms of the parish and the type of event before filtering by date.

Natural disasters have much overlap with researching accidents so the previous section still applies; however, there are some differences. Accidents often have a person whose fault it was that the incident occurred. Natural disasters can rarely be blamed for the event occurring itself; however, there may still be some blame for the aftermath. This could involve, for example, local councils being blamed for a lack of flood defence or firemen being blamed for a slow response. If there is an angle on the story where blame can be placed then people are more likely to be named.

Those named in stories about natural disasters are most likely to be those who died as a result of the event. Those who were severely injured or lost property may also be named, as well as witnesses and key local figures such as politicians, vicars and mayors. You may also find your ancestor named if they donated money or items such as clothing to people who had lost their home or belongings, or if they were involved in rebuilding the community.

In Britain we tend to have fewer major natural disasters, such as earthquakes, than other countries. You may be surprised, however, to find that your ancestor experienced something such as this, which would be an interesting fact to add to their life story. The article on the following page from *The Yorkshire Post and Leeds Intelligencer* on 30 April 1873 details an earthquake that occurred in Doncaster. Nobody is named in the article; however, the event would certainly have been something a person in the vicinity would remember.

We all have memories of major weather events that occurred within our own lifetimes. These may not be classified as natural disasters, but such events are still of interest. Try searching for your ancestor's parish of residence along with a relevant term to see what results appear. This could be anything from a storm to heavy snow.

Weather would have been hugely important to our forebears. Many of our ancestors were involved in agriculture. Too much or too little rain could be crucial to their crops and farmers would have been keen to read the latest forecasts, though these were much less accurate than today. Other occupations also needed to know the predicted weather, such as mariners, builders and fishermen. The first shipping forecast was published in 1859, followed shortly by the first official weather forecast which was published in newspapers in July 1861.

EARTHQUAKE AT DONCASTER.

An earthquake, of a sharper character than any that has been felt for some years, was experienced in Doncaster about twenty minutes to three o'clock yesterday afternoon. The sensation was an upheaving one, persons sitting at the time being suddenly jerked forward on to the tables before them, or even thrown bodily off their seats. So alarming was the phenomenon that people rushed out of their houses to inquire of one another the cause of the strange disturbance. One gentleman, formerly connected with the Great Northern Plant Works, living outside Doncaster, was so impressed with the belief that an explosion had occurred at the works that he had a horse saddled, and rode off post haste to ascertain whether such were the case. Many tradesmen had the goods in their shop disturbed ; furniture, in upper rooms especially, was visibly displaced, and crockery ware was audibly agitated. The undulation was much more perceptibly felt in one part of the town than another, and it is also to be remarked that people in upper storeys felt the shock whilst those below appeared to be quite unconscious that anything had happened. At the *Chronicle* and *Gazette* offices the disturbance was sharply felt, the whole of the compositors experiencing the rising and sinking sensation, which appears to have been its most distinctive characteristic.

A short report on a minor earthquake in Doncaster in *The Yorkshire Post and Leeds Intelligencer* on 30 April 1873. *(Content provided by the British Library Board. All rights reserved. With thanks to The British Newspaper Archive (www. britishnewspaperarchive.co.uk))*

It may be of interest to you to read about the weather for key dates in your ancestor's life. There is an article in *The Western Gazette* on 30 January 1931 about my great great-grandparents Walter Eli Hatcher and Elizabeth Osment's golden wedding anniversary. This states that when they married it was at the end of a large snowstorm which 'swept nearly all of England and Wales in January 1881'. On their wedding day, the snow is described as 'just thawing away', giving me lovely extra detail about what the day was like for them. The majority of couples will not have such an article written about the weather on their wedding day, but it may be of interest to search for the forecast or any weather events that occurred around the day.

The weather on other events may also be interesting to discover. Finding out that there was heavy rain on the day your ancestor was buried may not give you extra genealogical information to pursue; however, it does paint a clearer picture of what the funeral was like for their loved ones. Similarly, finding out it was freezing cold when your ancestor was born tells us how difficult it would have been for the mother to give birth in such conditions in days long before central heating. Newspapers frequently reported about the observations of the weather on previous days rather than forecasts.

If you find an article that names your ancestor as having been involved in a weather event or natural disaster, or if their parish or street is named as having been affected, think hard about how this would have impacted on them. This can lead to new discoveries. You may find that your ancestor lost their belongings in a property fire caused by a lightning strike. This may then lead you to find them named in the churchwardens' accounts for their parish as having been donated items such as fuel and clothing. Place yourself in their shoes and imagine how hard it would have been for them to rebuild their lives after such a loss. Think about whom they may have stayed with afterwards and if there was any other lasting effect. A distant cousin of mine was admitted to his local psychiatric hospital after losing his house in a fire and is reported on his admission to have been terrified about how he could provide for his children. Thankfully, the records show this was a short stay and later census returns show him living in a new property with his family.

Chapter 4

CRIMINAL AND COURT REPORTS

You may find your ancestor named in court reports. This could be in a criminal case as the accused, victim, witness or law official, or it could be in a different court such as a civil court or at a coroner's inquest. Bigger crime stories will be found in national newspapers as well as local newspapers, although both should be searched in case extra detail is provided in a particular title. Local newspapers also featured more minor local crime. The latter can really help you to understand more about your ancestor: whether they failed to register a birth within the required time frame; were fined for not sending their children to school; or if they were charged with spousal abuse.

Not all stories made it to the newspapers so if you are aware from another source that your ancestor was accused of or a victim of a crime, you may not be able to find a relevant article. Alternatively, if a newspaper article is the first time you have discovered that your ancestor was involved in a crime, you can use the information to trace other sources about the incident. This could involve prison registers, quarter sessions records and petitions, among other records. Some of these will be available online; others at county archives. Articles will give the date and place of the trial, which will help you search for a related record. If a crime occurred but nobody was brought to trial, it could be that a newspaper article is the only surviving source.

History of Crime Reporting

Newspapers have always featured a significant number of crime reports. To begin with, newspapers reprinted crime stories from London and major international crime stories. It was not until the nineteenth century that newspaper editors truly realised the potential selling power of publishing crime stories that were local to their readers. Understandably, people wanted to know what was happening around them. For major crimes, such as murder and rape, readers wanted to stay informed so they could keep themselves and their families safe. For more minor crimes, subjects were often used as a form of gossip among readers. Whatever the reason for their popularity, articles about scandalous or alarming crime have always helped to sell copies of newspapers.

The Quarterly Pursuit was first published in 1772 and after multiple name changes, including famously *Hue and Cry*, settled on its present name of the *Police Gazette* in 1839. The publication was free to readers until 1793. The paper contained the names and details of those of interest to the police, including army deserters, escaped convicts and those who were to be deported. There was also a supplement giving the names of those who had previously featured in the publication who had recently been confirmed dead.

Another specialist crime newspaper was *The Illustrated Police News*, which was published 1864–1938. This was not an official paper, rather one that simply focused on the scandalous stories from London and the rest of the world that it deemed to be of most interest to readers. The front page would feature an artist's impression of the criminal story of the time; this was often heavily exaggerated for maximum effect. Other illustrations appeared inside the publication, such as drawings of crime scenes and those charged with crimes. As well as stories of law breakers, the newspaper featured articles about natural disasters and tales from the battlefield.

Crimes were reported in a particularly graphic manner in the early nineteenth century. Those involving bloodshed were a particularly popular choice with journalists and readers alike. Stories that invoked fear in readers tended to result in repeat sales where readers were keen to find out more in the next issue. This desire to cause fear in readers is a method still used by sections of the media today to increase readership. You may see this in cases involving serial crime or contagious illnesses, particularly since the coronavirus pandemic.

The bigger criminal news stories such as Jack the Ripper (1888) and the Crippen Case (1910) took up multiple column inches. Jack the Ripper was so-called because of a hoax letter sent to the Central News Office in London; the name stuck. Prior to this publication, newspapers usually referred to the suspect as the Whitechapel murderer due to the location where the victims were found. Browsing the newspapers for prolific cases to see how they developed over time can be fascinating.

Many of our ancestors must have hoped to read that the Ripper had been caught and would have been mightily disappointed to know that the case still remains unsolved today. You can similarly trace the case of Dr Crippen, as previously mentioned, from his arrest to his trial and finally to his execution. This is a more satisfying read with a final conclusion.

Journalists have never been able to access all the information available to the police. If they wished to write a report on criminal activity, a journalist could speak to law enforcement on an informal basis. This was traditionally done by visiting pubs with the officers in the hope of gaining more information from them in a relaxed environment. Journalists could also speak to victims and witnesses to add more detail and colour to a report. While newspapers were happy at first to copy and paste other publications' stories, the competition between them soon grew and they wished to stand out by having exclusive information. From the twentieth century, journalists could attend a police press conference. Using this method, the police could release a pre-prepared statement with facts that they wished the media and public to know about. Conferences also gave journalists the opportunity to ask questions that they believed their readers would wish to know the answers to.

As printing technology evolved, newspapers became increasingly able to include illustrations and photographs with improved clarity and at a reduced cost. For stories involving crime, this was especially useful as drawings of suspects could be printed, as well as photographs of those implicated, maps of a crime scene and images of stolen goods. As photographs cannot be taken from inside a court room, this led to the emergence of courtroom sketches where a trained artist could quickly draw their impression of the defendant.

Criminal Court Reports

It is common to find an ancestor involved in a crime. In fact, it is much rarer to discover a person's tree with no links to a crime, whether that is as the accused, victim or witness. If you can find an article naming your ancestor in a court report, this could give you a great deal of useful information including, but not limited to, their occupation, address, age and marital status. More uniquely, court reports can give us a verbatim account of what our ancestors said. This opportunity to 'hear' our ancestors' words is one rarely found in other sources. These accounts can be very lengthy, particularly in the eighteenth and nineteenth centuries, whereas later on they are more succinct.

The first mention of a crime is often in a person's local newspaper. Depending on the type of crime and the circumstances, this may be at petty sessions, quarter sessions or assizes. The more minor crimes were heard at petty sessions with very serious crime heard at assizes. There were overlaps between the three courts. Theft, for example, may be heard at petty sessions or quarter sessions depending on the value of what was stolen. You will frequently see the term 'police court' used in newspapers. This is an inaccurate phrase referring to a magistrates' petty sessions court. The police do not operate courts.

If the crime was deemed to be of interest to readers outside the local area, it may be picked up by newspapers in neighbouring counties or nationwide. The biggest news stories were reprinted globally. Popular stories for newspapers to print would usually involve scandal such as murder due to an extra-marital affair, outrageous crimes such as those involving children, or crimes involving the celebrities of the day.

Not all crimes feature in newspaper articles. Even cases that made it to assizes did not always make it to the press. Minor crimes or those of little public interest often have one short article with no further follow-up. For crimes involving lengthy trials it is recommended that you read the articles as the news unfolded day by day rather than simply skipping to the end summary and verdict. This will help you to see how the trial developed. Despite newspapers often copying other publications' articles word for word, some journalists did make the effort to include extra information, so it is worth searching different titles to make sure nothing is missed.

Some cases feature in a summary under a shared heading. These will usually list the name of the person charged, the crime they were charged with and the sentence given. Sometimes extra detail is supplied such as their age or occupation and more information about the case is given with more serious crimes. A typical example from its time can be seen on the following page where a summary of cases heard at Stafford Assizes is given.

As previously mentioned, a popular heading is 'Police Court hearings'. These give a round-up of the most interesting cases of the previous week and can be found as a regular feature in both daily newspapers and weekly publications. If there is a particularly interesting case only this may feature with no others described.

Other cases of more public interest feature under their own headings. These examples will usually be found in multiple newspaper titles over a few days or weeks. As you would expect, these give more detail than the summaries, especially in terms of the nature of the crime committed. The defendant may be described in more detail, including their physical appearance, demeanour and any previous offences. The accused tend to receive more column space than their victims, but the latter may also

ASSIZES.

STAFFORD Affize commenced on Wednefday ; Lord Kenyon prefided at the *Nifi prius* Bar, and Baron Perryn at the Criminal Bar. Thomas Wilmot Oliver, charged with the wilful murder of Mr. Wood, by fhooting him on Friday the 27th day of January laft, was, after a trial of upwards of nine hours, found guilty, and fentenced to fuffer death this day, and his body to be delivered to the furgeons for diffection. A plea of infanity was brought forward, which was endeavoured to be proved hereditary ; and Drs. Johnftone and Arnold, who had examined Mr. O. in vain for him gave evidence tending to prove a mental derangement. In the diftraction occafioned by difappointed love, Mr. O. committed the crime for which he fuffers. The daughter of Mr. Wood was the object of his unfortunate affection.

J. Williams, for robbing Mr. Land, of Uttoxeter, of bills and cafh, was capitally convicted ; B. Alton, for ftealing brafs caps, &c. and Hannah Lane, alias Harper, for robbing Mr. Chinner, of Walfall, of a quantity of calico, are to be tranfported 7 years; Judith Allfop, and Ann Cooper, for a theft at Ingeftrie, are to be imprifoned 6 months; W. Cooper, charged with ftealing a Friendly Society's Box at Kingfwinford, A. Bailey and M. Gee, charged with ftealing Cotton, and G. Grant, with ftealing a horfe under pretence of hiring him, were acquitted. All the Prifoners were not tried at the time our account was fent from Stafford.

Report on Stafford Assizes in *Aris's Birmingham Gazette* dated 28 August 1797 giving detail about the murder trial of Thomas Wilmot Oliver followed by the lesser crimes of others. *(With permission from Archives and Collections, Birmingham Libraries)*

be described. These crimes may be reported in the area where the crime occurred as well as any newspapers local to where the defendant or victim lived, if this is different.

You may find a report on a trial involving your ancestor but be unable to find its conclusion published. This is, sadly, not uncommon and happened when court cases were adjourned or if other news stories simply took priority. There are times where you will not be able to find your ancestor named at all, despite knowing they were involved in a crime. This probably means the crime was not deemed interesting enough that week to report on. In other cases, it may be that it was published in a newspaper but the title has yet to be digitised. Children under the age of 18 could not be named in criminal cases from 1933 onwards unless a judge ruled it to be in the public's best interest.

There are numerous reports in newspapers surrounding crime where the accused is unknown. These are common in cases of breaking and entering, rape, street assault and muggings. In these cases, victims may be named and the locality it occurred will also be given. An address may help you confirm the identity of a victim. If your ancestor was charged later with these crimes it is worth searching back through the newspapers to read about how the crimes were reported at the time. This is tricky when you cannot search by name. Try searching local newspapers by date and using the address, area or crime as a search term. Crimes have always gone unsolved so many of us will have ancestors who committed crimes that we will forever be unaware of.

If you find an article of interest about your ancestor, whether as the accused, victim or other, ensure you follow this up with further records. These are most likely to be held at the local county archive; for example, if the crime was committed in Dorchester and reported in local Dorset newspapers any relevant documentation is most likely to be held at Dorset History Centre. Prison records can give you a more complete picture of what happened. A newspaper article may state that a person was sentenced to five months' imprisonment but prison registers may show they were let out early. The date of the court's verdict as supplied in newspapers is usually the same date that the defendant was sent to prison. This can help you to find them in prison admission registers.

The verbatim accounts provided by newspaper journalists may be the only chance we have to 'hear' what our ancestors had to say. Sometimes these can hint at an accent they had according to the spelling. These should be recorded accurately by the journalist, but remember in all cases what is being said may not be truthful. Defendants, victims and witnesses may all lie to sway a judge or jury. Nevertheless, you can learn a lot about a person's character from these accounts.

There may be additional information in the newspaper if your ancestor misbehaved while being imprisoned. People were held in gaols and prisons while they awaited their trial, as punishment in its own right, prior to transportation or before their execution. Whatever their reason for being held in a gaol or prison, you may come across evidence in newspapers of violence they inflicted upon other inmates or staff while there, or even an attempted or successful escape. In the *Kentish Gazette* on 26 December 1797, the escape of Elizabeth Whitbread from Dover Gaol on 20 December is described. A reward of 5 guineas is offered for her capture. As she was still at large, a physical description is provided; 'she is between 40 and 50 years of age, of a middling height, pale in the face and has a sickly emaciated appearance. She had on when she escaped an old black bonnet and wore an old whitish great coat over a short dirty linen gown.' Such descriptions were essential to help with the apprehension of an escaped inmate in times before photography. This is of great benefit to us and may well be the closest we get to knowing what our ancestors looked like.

The best example I have in my own family tree regarding crime in newspapers is that of my great great-grandfather Alexander Taylor (1865–1920). Alexander resided in Maidstone, Kent and had eight children with his wife Alice Rosa Colyer. By all accounts, Alexander was a prolific criminal appearing frequently in local newspapers. The first appearance was in January 1881 when aged 15 he was fined 5 shillings for larceny. The article notes this was not his first appearance in court. Three months later, he was charged another 5 shillings for throwing stones at a property. The article for this offence states that Alexander, even at this young age, showed no signs of wanting to reform. Sadly, this prediction came true with Alexander appearing in court and in newspapers for the rest of his life with offences including theft, assaulting a police officer, being drunk and disorderly, poaching, refusing to pay for beer, obscene language, obstructing the police, refusing to pay the fees for his son's reformatory school, trespass and assaulting his rent collector, among many others.

Clearly this is not an ancestor to be proud of. However, because of Alexander's abundant crimes I am able to discover more about him and his character from using local newspapers. Alexander's occupation appears to change very frequently, as well as his place of residence. He is described as a 'nuisance to police', 'a rough-looking fellow' and perhaps most interestingly 'an idle disorderly fellow whose wife went out to work and kept him and the children'. One Chief Constable even stated: 'there could not be a worse character going about than Alexander Taylor.'

By tracing newspaper articles naming Alexander Taylor, I am able to gain a much fuller picture of the man he was than using archival records alone. Searching newspapers for Alexander's crimes is also much quicker than browsing catalogues and prison registers. From the articles about him, I can use the dates to discover more about the charges against him much more efficiently than if the information had not been printed.

It is common to find family members named in criminal court cases such as Alexander's above. Family members were often called as witnesses or to give character testimonials. In other cases, a family member may have been involved in the crime, whether as an 'also accused' or as a victim. Members from the same family may have carried out a burglary together as accomplices, or they may have been on opposing sides in a bigamy or assault case. Court cases surrounding bigamy and affiliation orders often give very useful genealogical detail drawn from documentary evidence such as birth and marriage certificates, as well as witness statements from family members on all sides. With affiliation orders and bastardy cases you can discover the name of the reputed father of an illegitimate child where they are refusing to pay for its care. In these cases, the child is rarely named so it is best to search using the name of the mother if the father is unknown.

Crime Statistics

Generic crime statistics make frequent appearances in newspapers. Local newspapers report on crime in their area, whereas national newspapers usually focus on London, unless there has been a notable crime wave elsewhere. These do not name specific people but are of a general interest. Most are annual statistical reviews. If you are aware that your ancestor committed a certain crime or faced a certain punishment during a particular year you can view these figures to discover how many others were in the same position. You may find their crime and punishment were fairly commonplace or they may have been alone in their fate that year.

In *The New Times* on 17 March 1823 the statistics for Newgate Prison for 1822 are revealed. There were twenty-three executions, two deaths and hundreds of other prisoners removed to various locations, including prison hulks, refuges and Bethlem Hospital. Twenty-one were released having received a royal pardon and over 300 were acquitted at Old Bailey sessions. The punishments faced by those who were released are given, including those who were fined and whipped. Following this, another list is presented of the offences for which prisoners were convicted. This includes burglary, highway robbery, sheep stealing, fraud, embezzlement and selling blasphemous publications, among many others.

Yet another list gives the number of people sentenced to each punishment, including death, transportation, imprisonment for various terms, fines and whippings. The final list details the crimes of the twenty-three men who were executed that year. The most common crime resulting in execution in Newgate Prison in 1822 was burglary, resulting in ten inmates' deaths. This is followed by three for forged notes, highway robbery and stealing in a dwelling house to the value of 40 shillings and above, two for sodomy and one each for forgery and murder.

The discovery of such statistics can also help us to understand the world that our innocent ancestors lived in. Viewing changing crime statistics helps provide a context to the darker side of the country that our ancestors may have been, or were afraid of being, a victim. It can also raise moral questions viewing the types of crime that resulted in the death penalty and transportation.

Transportation

If your ancestor was sentenced to be transported, their name may appear in the newspaper. This is also true for those whose sentence was later reduced to imprisonment or hard labour. In most cases, their name will be given along with the length of their transportation sentence. You can see an example of this below.

CENTRAL CRIMINAL COURT, Dec. 6.

SENTENCES.

Left for Execution.—William Smith, alias Glennister.

Sentence of Death Recorded.—William **Harriss, Henry Round.**

TRANSPORTATION.

Ten Years.—William Johnson, Thomas William Mellish.

Seven Years.—John Lind, John White, Catherine Adams, Robert Fortescue Mackrell, James Douglass, George William Warman, Cornelius Mahony, Henry Robert Brown, George Todd, John Sands.

IMPRISONMENT.

Two Years.—Alexander Good.

Eighteen Months.—Joseph Smith, William Mason, Joseph Clinton, Thomas Ryan.

Twelve Months.—Henry Simpson, Sarah Williams, Christopher Reynolds, Thomas Bennett, John Simpson, Stephen Pigott, John Davidson, Eliza Shanley, William Willson, James Hart, Timothy Brennan, William Needs, William Rastall, John Smith, John Whitley, Mary Anne Pentoll, John Smith, Dennis Conway.

An excerpt from *Morning Advertiser* dated 8 December 1851 listing those sentenced to death, transportation and imprisonment along with the duration of their sentence. *(Content provided by the British Library Board. All rights reserved. With thanks to The British Newspaper Archive (www.britishnewspaperarchive.co.uk))*

In other cases, more detail is given such as the crime the person committed and what ship they sailed on. If you have found the name of the ship on which your ancestor was transported, it is worth researching in the newspapers to see if anything noteworthy appeared at the time of their travel. Transportation ships appeared in the shipping intelligence columns alongside other ships so you can see the date and place of the sailing and when and where they arrived. There are also some reports about the ill-treatment of convicts and terrible living conditions on board transportation ships. This includes articles about diseases, such as cholera, being reported as spreading through convicts and crew.

If the ship transporting the convicts sank this will feature, such as the ship *Waterloo* which sank in Table Bay, South Africa in 1842. In *The Morning Chronicle* on 16 November 1842, it was reported that among the deaths were 143 convicts, 15 soldiers, 14 sailors, 4 women and 14 children. Reading various reports about the wreckage gives varying numbers of the dead as well as the numbers of those who survived. Different accounts of the sinking appear in different newspapers showing the importance of reading several reports to gain a full picture of the event. Where accidents happen involving transportation ships, it is usually only some of the crew who are named; rarely are the convicts themselves named. If you know your ancestor was on board, whether they survived or not, reading about the event can help you understand what your ancestor witnessed.

The Death Penalty

Public executions were reported in great detail. As these were often very noteworthy criminal cases, the trial can often be followed throughout, including the verdict and the resultant hanging. One example is 25-year-old Frances Kidder, the last woman to be publicly hanged at Maidstone Gaol, in 1868. Frances was found guilty of drowning her 11-year-old stepdaughter, Louisa Kidder Staples. There are numerous newspaper reports of her criminal trial resulting in the death penalty. Viewing reports, you can see how Frances pleaded not guilty despite much evidence to the contrary. After the verdict was given, her execution date was set for 2 April 1868, with the first newspaper reports about the hanging being published on the same day. The first to report was the *Pall Mall Gazette*, an evening newspaper. This stated: 'The wretched woman went into hysterics and had to be supported on the drop by two warders. The crowd was small and orderly.'

The following day, 3 April 1868, newspapers all around the country had picked up the news. The case was summarised for the readers before the execution is described. In London's *Morning Post* that day a report is given rather contrary to that provided the previous day in the *Pall Mall Gazette*:

> She walked the whole of the distance from her cell to the scaffold with a firm step and mounted the steps leading to the gallows with but very slight assistance. Before the cap was put over her face she turned to the ordinary, who was deeply affected, and smiled, and the last words she uttered were 'Lord Jesus forgive me.' The drop then fell and after a short struggle life appeared to be extinct.

Reports of executions can make for rather grisly reading. The executions of five men, Arthur Thistlewood, Richard Tidd, James Ings, William Davidson and John Brunt, in 1820 after being found guilty of high treason as part of the Cato Conspiracy case are thoroughly described. While they were originally sentenced to be hanged, drawn and quartered this was later commuted to hanging and beheading. Multiple newspapers report the demeanour of each of the men and their last words, as well as giving gruesome descriptions of their deaths. *The British Neptune* on 8 May 1820 printed letters written by James Ings to his wife and children which, as well as naming multiple relatives, tell us a lot about his character.

" **P. S.** My dear wife, give my love to my father and mother, brother and sisters, and aunt Mary, and beg of them to think nothing about my unfortunate fate, for I am gone out of a very troublesome world, and I hope you will let it pass like a summer cloud over the earth.

" Newgate, four o'clock, Sunday afternoon, April 30, 1820.

TO HIS DAUGHTERS.

" To my dear Daughters,—My dear little girls, receive my kind love and affection, once more, for ever, and adhere to these my sincere wishes, and recollect, though in a short time, you will have nothing more of your father. Let me entreat you to be loving, kind, and obedient to your poor mother, and strive all in your powers to comfort her, and assist her whilst you exist in this transitory world, and let your conduct throughout life be that of virtue, honesty, and industry ; and endeavour to avoid all temptation, and at the same time put your trust in God. I hope unity peace, and concord will remain amongst you all. Fare-well, farewell, my dear children, your unfortunate father,

" To Wm. Stone Ings and his sisters. " JAMES INGS."

An extract from the letters that James Ings wrote to his wife and children prior to his execution, published in *British Neptune* on 8 May 1820. *(Public Domain)*

If you have an ancestor who received the death penalty, you may wish for somebody else to read the report before you in case you find the detail unsettling. Indeed, reading some of these reports can be unnerving to readers with no connection to the accused. Aside from the often-unnecessary detail of their deaths, you may be able to extract useful information. There is often a summary of the case supplied prior to their hanging. Their last words can give an insight into their state of mind, including any regret or insistence of their innocence. The behaviour of the crowd in public executions can hint whether the accused was viewed with hatred, curiosity or sympathy. It would be interesting to know whether our ancestors witnessed an execution; however, those in the crowd are very rarely named.

Bankrupts and Insolvent Debtors

Debt used to be considered as a crime in Britain. Prior to the Bankruptcy Amendment Act of 1868, debt was very common and debtors were the most common prisoners in the eighteenth and nineteenth centuries. A debtor could avoid being imprisoned if their property was taken by the courts and dispensed to the creditors. Until 1842, a person would be declared bankrupt if they owed over £100. Bankrupts and insolvent debtors can be found listed in both local and national newspapers. These notably appear in *The London Gazette*, as well as *The Edinburgh Gazette* and *The Times* between 1785 and 1985. Details given usually include the person's name, their place of residence and their occupation. Sometimes, the details of creditors are also supplied, as well as details about the debtor's imprisonment.

A specialist newspaper, *Perry's Bankruptcy and Insolvent Gazette*, was published from 1826, initially on a monthly basis before being published weekly from 1862. There are a variety of different headings in this paper, including 'Insolvents Applying to be Discharged' and 'Petitioning Creditors', which can make for interesting reading. Bankrupts used to be listed in the births, marriages and deaths column of some newspapers in the eighteenth century. You may also find some cases listed under a heading of 'Insolvent Debtors Court', such as in London's *Weekly Dispatch*, with cases summarised.

Civil Court Reports

Equity courts handled civil disputes. Topics could involve marriage settlements, contests of probate, custody cases and trading disputes, among many other issues. In England and Wales, the equity courts in London handled all civil disputes from around the country with people having to travel many miles to attend. In Scotland, the Court of Session handles both common law and equity cases. In both cases, equity court sessions may appear in newspapers. This is less common than a criminal court hearing, however, and usually equity cases will only feature if the topic is deemed to be of high public interest or if the people involved are well known to the public. You are more likely to find articles about equity court cases in the eighteenth and nineteenth centuries. Of particular use to us are cases regarding probate disputes. These reports can tell us that a named relative was deceased, the date that their will was written, who was named in the will and the names of those contesting it. The circumstances regarding the dispute can provide a great insight into family dynamics.

One civil court case example from the Court of Exchequer can be seen in London's *Weekly Dispatch* on 26 June 1853. The title of the case is provided as 'Pallett and Wife v. Hopkinson' which can help you find relevant records in The National Archives (TNA) catalogue where the records are held. The date of the hearing is 23 June. In a fairly lengthy summary, the article describes how the plaintiffs wished to recover monetary damages from the defendant who is named as the owner of a ship named *The Star*. Mrs Pallett is described as having received injuries at the fault of Mr Hopkinson who caused a collision while she was a passenger on board. She lost two teeth and suffered from concussion. The case was heard by Baron Martin and damages were awarded to the plaintiffs to the sum of £60.

Court of Chancery articles also provide the title of the case. In an example in *The Northampton Mercury* on 3 February 1798, the title of a case is given as 'Birch v. Birch and others'. The fact that the surnames are the same are a hint that the case surrounds a family dispute. In this example, the dispute surrounds a marriage settlement brought by a wife against her husband saying she had not received any annuities from him since 1789. The court ruled in favour of the wife.

In both these examples, you will notice that the full name of the plaintiffs and defendants are not provided. This is common in equity court case reports. This is an important issue to remember when searching for civil cases involving our ancestors, as searching for their full name will not bring up a result. If you are aware from searching in TNA catalogue that your ancestor was involved in a civil case use this to find the title of the case, i.e. 'Squibb v. Fry', and then use this as a search term. Alternatively, you can try searching using their surname and the word court, or the precise court, such as the Court of Chancery, if you know where their case was heard.

Coroners' Inquests

Coroner's inquests are public hearings which investigate the circumstances of a person's death. The majority of coroner's reports do not survive. This is frustrating to researchers when we are aware from an ancestor's death certificate that an inquest was carried out as so much information has been lost. Of those that have survived, we are only able to view reports after seventy-five years have passed, due to confidentiality. In both of these scenarios, newspapers can help. Whether the report itself has been destroyed or is being held privately, if a newspaper printed an article about the inquest then this will be searchable online. As coroner's inquests are public hearings, journalists have always been freely able to attend, therefore reports have featured in newspapers regularly since the mid-eighteenth century.

It is not always obvious if your ancestor's death would have warranted a coroner's inquest. They were held in cases of unexplained, sudden or suspicious deaths, including manslaughter and suicide. For deaths prior to civil registration in July 1837, we are not always aware of the cause of a person's death. After this time, if a death certificate mentions the word 'coroner' or 'inquest', usually in the informant column, it is worth first searching the local county archives for any surviving inquests and then to check newspaper reports. A newspaper article may be the only surviving source regarding the inquest.

The death certificate of my third great-grandmother Mary Jane Taylor (née Brown) gives her cause of death as natural causes. This is a common find for a cause of death, along with similar terms such as 'visitation of God' and 'old age'. None of these reasons tells us much about why our

SUDDEN DEATH.—An inquest was held on Wednesday on the body of Mary Jane Taylor (69), of Thornhill-place, who died suddenly on Sunday.—Evidence was given that she complained of feeling sick at dinner time and died shortly afterwards. Dr. Hill stated that deceased had an abscess in the right lung, and heart disease as well. It was wonderful she could go on at all that day. A verdict of " Death from Natural Causes " was returned.

The coroner's inquest report of Mary Jane Taylor from *Kentish Express and Ashford News* on 14 January 1905. (*Content provided by the British Library Board. All rights reserved. With thanks to The British Newspaper Archive (www.britishnewspaperarchive. co.uk)*)

ancestor died, how long they may have suffered or whether the death was sudden. In the informant column on Mary Jane's death certificate it is noted 'certificate received from Robert Hoar Deputy Coroner for Maidstone Inquest held 11 January 1905'.

Checking the Kent archives catalogue shows that, unfortunately, no coroner's inquest report has survived for Mary Jane. However, a search of the newspapers did give a result. The article on the previous page shows a summary of the inquest, including how Mary Jane died suddenly after feeling unwell at dinner time, had an abscess in her right lung and heart disease. Her age and address are also given, along with the date of the inquest.

The length of inquest reports in newspapers varies. Mary Jane's is short and to the point noting only necessary details. Others are much lengthier, especially in cases of manslaughter and murder where there was a greater public interest. Not all coroner's inquests found themselves in newspapers. Journalists often used inquests to fill space on a slow news day, so if your ancestor's inquest happened on the day of a big news story then it will be less likely to appear.

Articles about an inquest may give names of witnesses to the death or anyone else who was involved. This may include a doctor who prescribed medicine for the deceased or a neighbour who was the last person to see them alive. Policemen are frequently questioned and family members may also be named if this is relevant to the death. If the death was thought to be a possible suicide then numerous witnesses were called upon to gain an insight into the state of mind of the deceased. This can give a large amount of information with regard to the person's occupation, health, financial status, marital problems and any issues with the law. As suicide was an illegal act until 1961, it was important that the coroner discovered whether the cause of death was intentional or not. Verbatim reports from the witnesses and relatives may be provided which are of particular interest.

The reliability of statements given in an inquest can be questionable in many cases. As suicide was viewed upon so unfavourably, family members and friends were sometimes keen to try and persuade the coroner that the death must have been accidental. If the verdict was ruled a suicide then the deceased would not have been allowed a Christian burial on consecrated ground. In cases of murder and manslaughter the accused may try and argue their innocence. In all cases, the reliability should be questioned.

Suspected murder cases generally have the most column inches. The witness reports from murder inquests can be very insightful, especially where the deceased was killed by a spouse or family member. The details of their relationship are often thoroughly described, including the length of time they had been together, any abuse either of them suffered, any addictions either of them had, any children they had together or prior to their relationship and any issues they had mentioned to friends or relatives. It is often mentioned if a person had fallen out with their parents or in-laws or if their children were residing elsewhere. You can often get a very good idea of the state of a person's marriage from a murder case involving a spouse. Again, you must question the reliability of the statements given, particularly from the accused.

There are numerous inquest cases where the deceased is unnamed and unidentified. This may be because they are a vagrant and unfamiliar to the area or because the deceased had sadly been found so long after death occurred that they were no longer identifiable. This was especially common with deaths that occurred in the sea that washed up weeks later. If the inquest could not be certain of an identity then a name will also not be found on a death certificate.

Issues to Consider

Reading criminal and court reports in newspapers can raise a few issues with the reader. It is common to come across an ancestor accused of petty crimes, particularly those that were so minor they are no longer considered crimes today. It is still fairly common to come across a repeat offender or prolific criminal with regard to being drunk and disorderly in particular. With this in mind, we should remember the context of the crimes with which we are researching. Transportation was a common sentence for those accused of sheep stealing, house breaking and grand larceny. Even stealing clothes or food could result in transportation. Crimes were dealt with in a much harsher manner in the past than they are today, generally speaking.

Similarly, the mental health issues behind the reason for a person committing a crime were much less understood. This is why you may come across vulnerable people receiving a harsh sentence and being written about in a derogatory manner. This includes women who had recently given birth who we would now recognise as having postnatal depression and soldiers returning from the battlefield with what we would now know as post-traumatic stress disorder.

Historically, newspapers could paint people in an unfair light. An article about a woman who was a victim of a sexual assault may mention that she has an illegitimate child in a way that suggests this is relevant. If a person was a victim of a crime but had a previous unrelated conviction this may also be highlighted in an unfair manner. Some articles can make for very unpleasant reading, particularly where victims of crime have details of their home life mentioned unnecessarily.

When we are researching living people or those who have been recently deceased, we must remember to respect their privacy. A person may have committed a minor crime in their early twenties that they hoped had been forgotten about. They would never have thought about the possibility of newspapers being digitised and so easily searchable in the way they are today. It is advised in such cases not to make these articles viewable on a public tree and to keep them private unless the person themselves is happy for the information to be shared. There are also exceptions of confidentiality law. A victim of a crime, particularly if it was sexual in nature, may have had their name published at the time but later be protected by an anonymity order meaning you would be breaking the law by sharing this information. Remember also to research the story thoroughly in case a person charged with a crime was later found innocent. The proof of their innocence should be very clear on your tree.

Chapter 5

MILITARY NEWS

The reporting of military news goes back as far as the history of newspapers can take us. Initially, most early news sheets were solely about specific battles as discussed in Chapter 1. The accuracy and reliability of military reporting is and always has been dubious. British victories were often heavily reported and exaggerated whereas British losses were sometimes ignored completely. There have also been large periods of time where censorship has been necessary to avoid compromising military operations. This is particularly the case from 1915 onwards.

There are plenty of opportunities to find our ancestors named in newspapers with regard to their military career. This may be for a variety of reasons, including being caught as a prisoner of war, reported wounded, receiving a medal or being killed in action. Sometimes, details of a person's military career may appear in a newspaper at a later date, such as in an obituary, rather than at the time that they served. Alternatively, if a person is not named you may find details of what their regiment was doing at the time they served. This may include activities outside of wartime such as processions, dinners or training.

Battle Reporting

If you are aware that your ancestor fought in a particular battle, you can browse the newspapers to see how this was reported at the time. It is advisable to browse according to the date of the battle, because the name as we know it today may have been coined at a later time. Some news reports of battles took several days to reach British newspapers so keep extending your search until you discover the correct conflict.

Your ancestor is highly unlikely to be named in a news report such as this. These are, however, useful to us as researchers to find out what our ancestors at home were reading about the war that their loved ones were involved in. The reports can then be used to compare with more accurate descriptions of the battle to see how truthful the initial article was. For example, the Battle of the Somme began on 1 July 1916 and lasted until mid-November. It was devastating for British troops with the loss of 19,240 soldiers. However, two days after the battle began, a report in the *Staffordshire Sentinel* described the battle as having 'magnificent results' although they expected it to 'last for some days'. Battle accounts can be read for the following weeks and months to see how the tone of reporting changed over the period.

You may have more luck finding an ancestor named if they held a senior position and if they were killed or wounded. For example, after the Battle of Graspan on 25 November 1899 during the Boer War the details of several officers who were killed or wounded were given in *The Lancashire Daily Post* two days later. Alongside these details were illustrations of Commander Alfred Peel Ethelston who was killed in the attack and Captain Reginald Prothero who was wounded. The service careers of both are summarised.

The Press Association War Service Telegrams service published notifications of ongoing updates from the British and French sides during the First World War. These sometimes detail battles, surprise attacks and raids on enemy trenches, and at other times mention simple details like the weather. In *The Orkney Herald* on 8 November 1916, several notifications are made. It states that an enemy trench was captured east of Gueudecourt with further raids on enemy trenches near Arras, whereas news from the Ancre simply says heavy rain fell overnight with nothing special to report. If you know where your ancestor was serving on a particular date, it is worth searching for this place name to see what crops up.

Medals and Promotions

If your ancestor was awarded a medal, award or honour their name should appear in *The Gazette* and probably their local newspaper also. These lists tend to give their service number, rank, regiment, name using their first initial and the medal they were awarded. The lists can be seen appearing during wartime very frequently.

When awarded a medal or given a promotion, local newspapers may also note if they have any other family members serving with their regiments. These are usually brothers but may also be a father or son. If they had an ancestor who was previously highly regarded in the forces they may also be named, usually a father or grandfather.

Particularly prestigious awards will have lengthier articles in local as well as the national press. Men awarded the Victoria Cross often have the citation for their award given, sometimes with a brief outline of their military career. *The Scotsman* on 30 June 1915 notes the reasons for each of the ten men receiving a Victoria Cross, including Private John Lynn of the Manchester Fusiliers who 'handled his machine gun with very great effect against the enemy … although almost overcome by deadly fumes'. John died the following day from gas poisoning.

Named Servicemen

If you are hoping to find your military ancestor named in a newspaper there are certain scenarios where this is more likely. Casualty lists were published that named those who were wounded, taken as a prisoner of war or killed. These usually give little information other than the man's regiment, rank, name with the first name normally given as an initial and sometimes their service number. For example, in the *Folkestone, Hythe and District Herald* on 23 July 1942, Privates H.J. Brooks and C.H. Ellis are reported to have died, and Privates G. Collier and E. Scott are noted to have died while held as prisoners of war. Provincial newspapers reported on the deaths of soldiers from their locality, sometimes with lengthy obituaries and a photograph. These sometimes appeared a month or two after the serviceman's decease. Local newspapers also placed notices regarding injured soldiers. My great-grandfather William Eggelton (named in the report as Pte. Eggleton) was reported to have been gassed in France and removed to hospital in Southport in February 1918. His former employer is named in the article.

You are most likely to find your military ancestor named upon enlistment, particularly during the First World War. Local newspapers prided themselves on listing the names and regiments of those in the vicinity who had enrolled. Many published regular listings of all men who were currently serving. In these cases, little information is given, with details usually fashioned as: 'Pte. Holland, Royal Bucks Hussars'. At other times, statistics were published of how many men were serving in each parish. Names and figures of those who had been discharged or transferred were also circulated.

Most regiments published a journal, usually quarterly, with obituaries of officers, the names of those leaving service and general articles about life within the regiment. Copies can usually be found within regimental museums and some are still being published today. *The Green Tiger* is the journal of The Royal Leicestershire Regiment and has been published since 1904. Copies can be viewed for free online at

Deserters' names were frequently published, with the offer of a reward for helping capture them. These tend to give the man's name, age and last known address. These may be seen in local papers or in official publications such as the *Police Gazette*. A typical example can be seen below in the *Police Gazette* dated 26 September 1916. This list gives detailed information about each deserter, including their name, age, height, corps, place of birth and hair and eye colour. During wartime, the *Police Gazette*'s main focus was on deserters and stragglers, including those recently captured. The subsequent court case may also be reported when a deserter was found. This should state if the soldier gave himself up or was captured.

Photographs of servicemen are usually a head and shoulders shot. These tend to only be published if the person was awarded a newsworthy medal, was taken as a prisoner of war or if they were killed. Local newspapers sometimes published several photos of regular soldiers, usually as a morale boost. Newspapers wanted to name as many people as possible in an attempt to sell copies to family members and boost sales. During the Second World War, the *Bromley & West Kent Mercury* advertised for readers to send in their photographs of servicemen along with a brief biography. This is now a

Office No.	NAME.	Reg. No.	Corps.	Age	Height	Com-plxn.	Hair.	Eyes.	Trade.
209	Gregory, John A.	19386	Dpt Nts&DbyR	21½	5 3	—	—	—	coal miner
210	Grimmer, James	191096	In.WtrTrnsRE	39	5 5½	—	—	—	fireman
211	Gronow, Wm. J.	12935	3rdS.WalesBds	29½	5 8½	fresh	brn	brn	labourer
212	Gubbins, F.	8596	W. Yorks R.	29	5 5½	fresh	dark	blue	—
213	Hadnett, Cecil G.	36288	R. Garrison Art	24½	5 10	fresh	black	brn	butcher
214	Haigh, A.	14778	Dpt N. Lanc' R	21½	5 6½	fresh	brn	brn	warehsmn
215	Haley, Michael	11308	3rd Irish Gds	32½	5 9½	—	—	—	labourer
216	Hall, —	39895	21st ReBty RFA	28	5 6½	—	—	—	carman
217	Hall, R.	21652	10th R Ir. Fus	26	5 6½	—	—	—	stager
218	Hall, Silas	9550	3rd S. Staffs R	21½	5 6½	dark	dk brn	grey	horse drivr

An extract from the deserter's list in the *Police Gazette* dated 26 September 1916. Further columns list enlistment date and place, place of birth, date and place of desertion and any distinguishing marks, such as tattoos, moles and scars. *(Content provided by the British Library Board. All rights reserved. With thanks to The British Newspaper Archive (www.britishnewspaperarchive.co.uk))*

fantastic resource for genealogists. On 12 April 1940, the photographs and biographies of four local men are shown; three are members of the RAF and the other an army soldier. Their mini biographies give their military background, sporting achievements, names of relatives, schools they previously attended and their place of residence. As is usually the case with servicemen, their names are given as their rank, first initial and surname, such as 'Cpl. A Pettifor' which is worth bearing in mind when carrying out a search for a serviceperson. When searching for servicemen in newspapers, you can also try searching for their service number rather than their name to see if this brings up any results. This can help with any surnames which have been misspelt or transcribed incorrectly.

On rare occasions, soldiers sent letters home or directly to newspapers which made it to print, reporting on particular battles or on war life in general. While these letters could not disclose specific information, they can still be rather eye-opening as to what the writer was going through and where their thoughts lay. In *The Atherstone News* on 19 March 1915, a letter that Lieutenant Dalgliesh sent to his uncle, Mr W.S. Allen, made it

The death notice of Private W.T. Taylor in *The Coventry and Warwickshire Graphic* on 8 November 1918 featuring a brief biography and photograph. *(printed with permission from Coventry Archives)*

to print. This begins with a request to send him cigarettes, stating 'some of the poor beggars haven't had a smoke for four days'. The letter then goes on to describe some of the living conditions: 'I am fairly near the firing line and the big guns are banging away all around me. There is a very big one a few hundred yards away. They call it Grandma.' Lastly, he describes how the soldiers are billeted in farmhouses and states he hasn't slept in a bed since he left England. The discovery of a letter from an ancestor can be an invaluable insight into their mind.

Military News from Home

Newspapers can enlighten us as to how recruitment campaigns were used. From the beginning of the First World War, appeals appeared in columns stating: 'Your country needs you. It is the duty of all able-bodied young men to place their services at the disposal of Lord Kitchener.' Newspapers also show how advertising changed during wartime, with appeals to work for industries that contributed to the war effort, again with the by-line: 'Your country needs you.' Poetry was also a regular feature, generally with the aim to encourage men to enlist or to inspire optimism at home.

Tribunals regarding conscription can be highly informative. You may discover an ancestor who argued against medical advice with regard to whether or not he was fit to fight or ancestors who were conscientious objectors. The latter appear frequently in court. Those who held strong religious beliefs against taking part in any war activity, such as Quakers, particularly upheld their position and were willing to face multiple punishments for doing so. There were many other reasons why a man would refuse to fight. In *The Derby Daily Telegraph* on 20 June 1917, the case of 40-year-old Albert Hardy of Newbold was described. Albert explains to the court at Chesterfield that he put in a claim to the Law Society for exemption as he owned a 'one-man business'. He had not yet heard back and so had not enlisted. Despite strong arguments, such as giving examples of men in similar situations to him who did not have to go to war, the magistrate ruled against him. Albert was handed over to the military authorities and 'left under escort for the Drill Hall'. You may have found previous evidence of your ancestor enlisting but be unaware that they resisted this until you find such an article.

News regarding military action on British soil was heavily censored. In the Second World War, the Germans were not always sure where exactly their bombs had hit and the British obviously did not want to give them any information about this. Local newspapers can still be a good source of information about air raids, but this was normally published long after the event. Any news about it published at the time was usually kept very vague.

There are, as there so often are, exceptions to this rule. My grandfather Robert Eggelton was a soldier with the Royal Corps of Signals and was stationed in Eastbourne on 3 April 1943, the day bombs fell on the town. He was walking through the town centre when the air-raid sirens began to wail. After ignoring the warning, an air-raid warden directed him to the nearest surface shelter on Spencer Road. He again ignored this direction but the decision was to save his life. The shelter suffered a direct hit and was destroyed, killing everyone inside. After reading this story in his diary, I was surprised to find the incident was reported quite heavily in the newspapers the following day. In the *Eastbourne Gazette* on 7 April 1943, the air raid made front-page news with lengthy description of the Spencer Road bomb among the many others that had hit the town. The *Eastbourne Chronicle* on 10 April 1943 also noted the bombs that had hit and described the people who perished.

Newspapers can show us what our ancestors were reading at the time of war. During the Second World War, notices were placed showing how to use a gas mask. There are also notifications of meetings held by officials regarding air-raid precautions. There are also many crime reports where opportunists thieved and assaulted others during the necessary blackouts every evening. The blackouts also resulted in many unfortunate accidents involving car accidents and drowning where the hazard could not be seen in the dark.

You can find many adverts for land girls, often requesting the ability to drive a tractor to assist on the farm. There are also adverts aimed at farmers themselves, notifying them of land girls available in their area. Such an advert appeared in the *Welsh Gazette* on 8 April 1943 stating a number of land girls were available for potato planting with farmers requested to apply via the agricultural offices at Lampeter. If your ancestor was a land girl and you know where she worked, you may be able to find an advert that refers to her such as this, albeit not by name.

Militia

Your ancestor may have been balloted to serve in the militia. This was often referred to as the 'supplementary militia' to distinguish it from the local militia. A series of Militia Acts between 1757 and 1762 reorganised all counties' militia regiments using elements of conscription. Each parish was required to provide a set number of able-bodied men aged 18–50 for training, reduced to 45 in 1762. As there were not enough volunteers, a ballot system was used. A militiaman's role was based in Britain rather than overseas, with

Military News • 57

duties including coastal defence and guarding prisoners of war. The militia could also be called upon at any time to help with national emergency or to assist the police. Conscription via the ballot system was suspended in 1829 due to its unpopularity with the public, with the last list made in 1831. After this date, the militia recruited men through volunteering only.

During peacetime, militiamen were required to attend training for around 3–4 weeks each year. Details were printed in local newspapers. A representative example can be seen in *Aris's Birmingham Gazette* on 15 May 1797 which states that the Shropshire Supplementary Militia were due to meet at the Shire Hall in Shrewsbury at noon the following day to be 'trained and exercised for twenty days'. Anybody who did not attend was to be 'deemed a deserter' and fined £20. If this was not paid the man would be 'committed to the common Gaol, there to remain without Bail or Mainprize, for the space of six months, or until he shall have paid the said penalty'. Needless to say, attendance was taken very seriously.

Desertion from the militia was common. Lists of deserters were placed in the local press. In the *Hereford Journal* on 30 May 1798, the list of those who had deserted from the Herefordshire Supplementary Militia took up a column and a half. This gives their names and their parish, such as John Brown of Peterchurch and John Vaughan of Shobdon. For many, their occupation is also given. In other newspapers, descriptions of the deserters are given. In *The Norfolk Chronicle* on 20 August 1803, a table is drawn up listing the deserters' names, ages, height, hair and eye colour, birthplaces, occupations, date of enrolment and the date of desertion.

Information about militia regiments was published routinely in *The Gazette*. There are further articles about annual training as well as

Names of Deserters.	Age	Size.		Description.			Where Born.		Occupations
		ft.	in.	hair.	eyes	comp.	Town.	County.	
Rowland Kemp,	28	5	5	light	grey	fair	St. Ives	Hunts.	bricklayer
Thomas Gaylor,	29	5	4	dark	grey	pale	St. Benedict Cambridge	Camb.	whitesmith
Thos. Sculthorpe,	25	5	5	dkbr	br.	swar.	Eltisley	Do.	labourer
John Smith	32	5	10	.br.	ha.	brown	Mepal sead	Do.	Do.
John Cox,	26	5	5½	bl.	dkbr	swar.	Berkhampst	Herts.	Do.
Joseph Jones,	26	5	6⅓	lt.br.	haz.	pale	Baldock	Do.	taylor
John Compton,	28	5	9	br.	grey	dark	Hertford	Hertford	harness-ma
Charles Webb,	21	5	10½	dkbr	do.	brown	Lakenheath	Norfolk	labourer

List of deserters from the Cambridgeshire Militia featured in *The Norfolk Chronicle* on 20 August 1803. Further columns note their date of enrolment and date of desertion. (*Content provided by the British Library Board. All rights reserved. With thanks to The British Newspaper Archive (www.britishnewspaperarchive.co.uk)*)

announcements of the appointments of officers. For example, on 17 June 1788 it is stated that Thomas Morris has been promoted to lieutenant of the Dorset Militia.

Other

Details of regimental processions are often noted, particularly where they were part of a military funeral. These reports may be vague or they may give specifics, such as the order different regiments appeared in the procession and the route that they took. An article may appear before a procession, informing the public in case they wished to attend, or after the event describing what happened. You may find your ancestor's regiment involved in a procession but it is usually impossible to know whether they themselves took part.

Grand occasions, such as military dinners, are reported on. Usually, only senior military figures are named but others may appear, for example if somebody was given an award during the event. One example appears in the *Lichfield Mercury* on 10 July 1896 when the warrant officers, staff-sergeants and sergeants of the 1st Battalion South Staffordshire Regiment held their annual dinner the previous Friday. The report names previous and current members of the regiment by their military position, surname and parish, such as Sergeant Blackburn of Lincoln and Sergeant Fothinere of Lichfield. The opening speech made by the chairman, Sergeant Major Birch, is detailed. This includes the notification of the death of a former member of the regiment, Sergeant Major Scott, whose military career involved being 'a prisoner of the Russians for six months' and was awarded the 'French Legion of Honour for conspicuous bravery'. The speeches of many others are summarised, generally giving a brief history of their military background.

When browsing the newspapers during times of conflict, you will come across numerous miscellaneous articles relating to war. These can be eye-opening in either a heartwarming or heartbreaking way. A lovely article in *The Surrey Advertiser and County Times* on 23 September 1916 sees Lieutenant Colonel H.P. Treeby of the East Surrey Regiment sending his thanks for the receipt of gifts for his soldiers. Most of the gifts are monetary with the names of the donors given. Miss Elliott of Godalming sent two mufflers, whereas Mrs G. Byrne of Kingston gave two pairs of socks, two vests, two pairs of pants, twelve handkerchiefs, four toothbrushes, six candles, six tins of potted meat and one packet of chocolate.

Whatever military event you are searching for, be mindful of the dates you are searching within. If you are trying to find out about a battle or air raid during the Second World War widen your search to several years after the event. Newspapers frequently posted articles on anniversaries of the event in question, by which time they were less restricted by enforced censorship. This means you may find details of those killed or injured in attacks, along with photographs taken after the event, including bomb damage.

Non-Military Ancestors

As well as discovering the news of our military ancestors, we can also use newspapers to read about others who were involved during times of conflict. These include witnesses to attacks and medical personnel. There are many reports on medical personnel working in Britain and abroad, although again individuals are only named in extreme cases. Florence Nightingale is the most obvious example, featuring in numerous reports during and after the Crimean War. One elaborate article can be seen in *The Examiner* on 28 October 1854 and subsequently copied into many other newspapers. This lengthy feature names her family and details her working career at length. The majority of doctors and nurses go unnamed, sadly.

Witnesses to military attacks are frequently named with descriptions of what they saw. Evidence of this can also be found elsewhere in newspapers in surprising places. For example, in the *Nantwich Chronicle* on 28 June 1947, there is a notification of the marriage of Kenneth Glover to Christine Bradshaw. It is mentioned that Kenneth witnessed the dropping of the atom bomb in Nagasaki while working on the Siam–Burma railway. Remember that where witnesses' descriptions are provided these may be heavily censored during times of war.

Even if you do not have a serviceman ancestor within your family tree, reading the newspapers can show us the issues different wars would have caused them. Reports on the daily task of blacking out their houses in the Second World War, taking cover in shelters from air raids and growing their own vegetables can all inform us how life during wartime changed our ancestors' lives.

Chapter 6

ADVERTISEMENTS AND CLASSIFIEDS

The very earliest editions of newspapers carried advertisements as a way of generating revenue. This rapidly increased with newspapers realising the potential monetary gains from this and those placing the adverts themselves knowing their notice would reach a potentially large readership. Other forms of advertising, such as posters and leaflets, did not have the same level of circulation. The placing of so many adverts allowed the costs of newspapers to drop substantially, broadening their readership even more so. Newspaper adverts were often crucial to a business, whether this was a large, well-known company placing an advert in a national newspaper or a small business placing an advert in a local paper. In our ancestors' day they obviously could not advertise by methods we use today, such as on television or the internet, and newspapers were the best way to get their messages across.

As well as business advertising, classified adverts were a huge feature of a newspaper. These were either charged by the word or by the line depending on the newspaper title and as a result were usually kept quite short. This was an affordable way for our ancestors to advertise their need for something – whether that was a need to sell a property, to find a job or to locate a lost item, among others. Classified adverts could take up several pages of a newspaper. Those placing classified adverts often kept their names abbreviated, such as 'please contact R. Morris' rather than 'Richard Morris'. Bear this in mind when searching. In some cases, names are not even given and only a phone number or address may be provided. The latter could therefore be used as alternative search terms. These classified adverts have now largely disappeared, with people using modern job listings, online estate agents and social media instead.

As you browse through newspapers, you will notice how advertising of all types has changed. Business adverts became larger, with bolder text and eye-catching imagery. Classified adverts commonly used to appear on the front page before being relegated to the middle or back. There are various reasons for this. Stamp Duty placed a great restriction on the space available in newspapers and greatly limited the number of pages they could have. Adverts were usually therefore kept small and succinct. There were also printing limitations with regard to illustrations and photographs, the latter of which were not used until the mid-1800s.

Many newspaper websites allow you to filter by 'advert', but be aware this is not completely foolproof. The results will likely eliminate relevant results and retain irrelevant articles. This is a useful feature if you wish to have a general browse of advertising features, rather than searching for a specific business.

Business and Product Advertisements

You may be interested to view adverts from your ancestors' businesses and particular products that they sold. These may give a price for certain products that they are selling or simply tell you more about your

Servicing – Repairs – Crypton Tuning

Tyres – Ignition Fault Finding

RCC RODS CAR CARE

11 Plough Estate, Blandford Forum

Dorset DT11 7UG

Tel: (0258) 456323

Mobile: 0860 254467

Electronic Wheel Balancing – Welding

A transcription of an advertisement for Rod's Car Care, my father's mechanics business in Dorset, as seen in the *Daily Echo* on 29 August 1991.

ancestor's business, including its location. Even the more contemporary adverts can be of interest. On the previous page is a transcription of an advert for my father's mechanics business from 1991. This shows the company logo, the address of the business, his phone numbers and details some of the tasks he carried out.

If you cannot find an advert relating to your ancestor's business you may wish to view other advertisements from the same time period to gain a better idea of their role. The services offered and costs may differ slightly but if nothing else it can show you who their local competition was. Where they are found, an advert can be a fantastic tangible aspect to your family history. This is true even if your ancestor was an employee of a large company rather than a business owner. If you decide you wish to print your ancestor's life story, a decorative advert can really bring this to life and hold the reader's interest.

If your ancestor was not involved in a business, adverts can still be very informative to read. You can get an idea of how much they would have been paying for particular items and services, the type of marketing that was used at the time and the sometimes outrageous claims that were made. In our ancestors' day, claims made in advertisements were not regulated, meaning those placing an advert could state whatever 'fact' they liked. This includes claims of magical concoctions curing apparently incurable illnesses, and products that never break.

Retailers and manufacturers knew who to pitch their adverts to and were not afraid to stereotype. Products for the home, such as vacuum cleaners and baking merchandise, were aimed at women, particularly mothers. You can discover many sexist and ageist adverts which would not be allowed to be published today. These adverts were worded to

An advert for men's Lava soap aimed at women, seen in *Tonbridge Free Press* on 22 September 1944. *(Content provided by the British Library Board. All rights reserved. With thanks to The British Newspaper Archive (www.britishnewspaperarchive.co.uk))*

appeal to women, stating products could help them save time with cooking or cleaning. Some were aimed at men to buy the same products for their wives; gifts that may not have been well received!

The first classic box advertisement appeared in *The Daily Telegraph* in the late 1850s. By 1900 these were commonplace. You will find that the information supplied in business advertising varies wildly. Some businesses placed an advert of a few words, such as 'Saxa: The Best Packet Salt', with no further information. Others try to sell their products by giving as much detail as possible, including what materials or ingredients the product is made from, the price, where it can be purchased and why their product is better than any competition. Be aware that if you are searching for a particular term, such as a company name, and this happens to be embedded within an image such as a company logo, this is unlikely to be picked up as a result by OCR.

You can also discover advertisements for new inventions, sometimes taking on more of an appearance of a news article. At other times you will find 'patent inventions' for sale by those who have invented something but do not have the time, skill or inclination to take it any further. Such articles may name your ancestor as the creator or give their home or business address. The majority of such placements can be found in the late nineteenth century.

Situations Vacant Advertisements

You may discover an advertisement placed by an ancestor looking for an employee. Alternatively, if you know the name of your ancestor's manager, you may be able to find the job advert placed prior to their employment. These adverts tend to appear under the heading of 'Situations Vacant' or 'Help Wanted'. There are many examples where advertisements such as this are placed under the 'Situations Wanted' heading instead of 'Situations Vacant'. These will still appear under a general search, so long as you do not insist that 'vacant' is a necessary search term.

Some of these notices are of very little help. One such notice appeared in *The Dorset County Chronicle* on 21 April 1910, with the advert simply stating: 'A boy wanted – apply 33 Glyde-path Road, Dorchester'. It is hard to believe anyone would reply to such an advert with no further detail. Other adverts give plenty of detail. The details of the job are usually given, the place of work is sometimes, but not always, supplied and salary may be mentioned. The person or company placing the advert is not always given.

You can also see the changing attitudes in the local adverts placed by our ancestors where people would request that only a person of a specific age and sex could apply. A notice placed in *The Caernarvon &*

WANTED, in small family, strong, willing GIRL. Comfortable home. Wages £12—Mrs Haile, Purton Farm, near Blakeney
o7252

WANTED, at once, respectable GIRL, about 16, to help with children and do a little light housework. Comfortable home. Another servant kept—Mrs Taylor, High-street, Ledbury 5636n

WANTED, COACHMAN ; married, no family ; drive single-pair ; good rider ; £1 week ; lodge, garden, coals—Mrs Sanderman, Crickhowell
o7181

COACHMAN Wanted ; married, no family ; thoroughly up in all duties ; drive pair. Groom kept. House, garden, coal found—Age, height, weight, wages and all particulars to le Tymawr, Abergavenny
5698n

WANTED, GROOM-COACHMAN ; drive single, double, and ride well. Cottage found. Abstainer preferred—Apply, stating age, whether married, and wages—T. R. Oswald, Milford Haven 5674n

WANTED, GROOM-COACHMAN (to live in) ; livery found. Must ride and drive well and turn out clean and smart—Apply, stating age, wages required, and experience, to E. M. Leir, Cwmgcedwig, Llanfarian, Aberystwith
-2235

A typical example from the 'Situations Wanted' column of *The Hereford Times* on 30 March 1901 with employers' names and address given. There are requests for employees of a specific sex and age with requests for their height and weight on application. (*Content provided by the British Library Board. All rights reserved. With thanks to The British Newspaper Archive (www.britishnewspaperarchive.co.uk)*)

Denbigh Herald on 18 August 1883 requests a groom and gardener who had to be unmarried and applicants were to provide their age, height and weight. This is not an uncommon find. Many adverts require their potential employees to be unmarried in their late teens or early twenties, with some adverts in the early twentieth century even requesting their candidates should submit a photograph of themselves along with their application.

You may discover your ancestor placed an advert requesting help at home. A typical advert can be seen in *The Yorkshire Post* on 19 July 1920: 'Mother's help wanted, August, fond of children: two maids kept – Apply Mrs B. Aplin, North Ferriby E. Yorks'. As well as mothers requesting assistance, it is common to find elderly widows and widowers requesting household help and company.

Situations Wanted Advertisements

Those looking for work could place an advertisement in a newspaper to see if there was any interest. These are normally found under the heading of 'Situations Wanted'. These sometimes give the person's name, although often only in initials, and the position they are looking for. They usually highlight a particular skill and may give personal details, such as their age. Some are very minimal. In *The Herald* of Wallington & Carshalton on 4 December 1886 an advert states: 'Cooking or Washing by the Day or Week – Mrs H. D. 1 Caledon Road, Carshalton'. In this case you are obviously only going to get a result if you search by your ancestor's address. Others give more detail. In the *Sussex Agricultural Express* on 23 June 1891 a notice states: 'As Coachman, Second Horseman, or Phaeton Groom; country preferred; good stableman; understands hunters, ride and drive well single or pair; excellent character; single, age 25, weight 9st. 7lb. Address, F Rout, 42 Dillwyn-street, Ipswich, Suffolk.' Here in one notice you have the man's name, work experience, marital status, age, weight and address. There are numerous examples, however, where the person's name and address are not given, with the recipient requested to reply to a certain box number of the newspaper for privacy reasons. If you find an advert naming an ancestor, remember this does not necessarily mean that they found the position they were looking for. Further sources will need to be located to discover this, such as census returns, trade directories and civil registration records.

Property Listings

If your ancestor wished to sell their property or rent it to tenants they may have placed an advert in their local newspaper. Provincial newspapers had 'Property to Let' and 'Property for Sale' sections in the classifieds where readers could browse for houses, occupational buildings and land that might be of interest. These were commonly sold at auction, with the date, time and place of the auction given in the advertisement.

Property listings can name the owners wishing to sell or let, as well as the names of any departing tenants. Addresses may be given and some state the name of a previous owner along with the fact that they are recently deceased. At times, no names or addresses are given – which, unfortunately, makes identification impossible. The important features of the property are given; often the entire layout of a house is described along with the acreage of any land and descriptions of outbuildings. The reason for sale may be given and the suggested sale price or requested rent can give a financial insight.

Property listings date back to the eighteenth century. These were not found in their own column section but were interspersed among other advertisements. Many of the property listings, unfortunately, only name the auctioneer or solicitor involved in the sale. This would be of interest to those researching the occupational history of their auctioneer or solicitor ancestors, but would be very difficult for the descendant of the property owner to find.

You may have luck with twentieth-century newspapers when searching by your known ancestor's address. This could be when they bought or sold a property. In Sheffield's *Telegraph and Independent* on 16 May 1939, an advert states: 'Crosspool (47 Barholm Rd) – Modern semi-detached house for sale: owner leaving city'. This result could help somebody pinpoint the time at which their ancestor moved away from Sheffield. Others state the owner is deceased or moving abroad. Similarly, if the advert regards an occupational plot such as a blacksmith's shop or an inn, this may help you date when your ancestor changed their occupation or at least the location of their work.

Personal Advertisements

Placing a notice in a local newspaper to meet similar-minded locals in your area for friendship or a potential romantic relationship has gone out of fashion since the internet made this quicker and easier with a broader readership. Personal 'ads', otherwise known as a 'lonely hearts' or 'matrimony' column, date back to the eighteenth century and are often quaint and humorous to read. The earlier the personal ad, the more likely it was to be placed by a wealthy gentleman seeking a partner of a similar status. Unfortunately, due to the sensitivity of the topic and privacy concerns, names are almost always omitted. This means we cannot know the identity of the person who placed the advert, with respondents asked to reply to a newspaper box address. The need for secrecy and privacy is often highlighted. Nevertheless, personal ads can teach us about the language used during courting at the time and the difference in attitudes compared to today.

Many earlier adverts request that only people with certain hair colours, eye colours, heights and other aspects of physical appearance respond, as well as some highlighting the respondent should be amenable to global travel, play the piano and speak foreign languages. The author often states he comes from good pedigree and quotes his annual income. Later adverts are much less fussy, with the writer appealing more for similar interests to themselves rather than specific talents or traits. Some give identifiable information, which may hint that it could be your ancestor. For example, some state they have lost fingers, recently been widowed or have just turned 30, but it would be very hard to trace your ancestor this way. Most personal ads were placed by men, especially in the eighteenth and nineteenth centuries.

Live Music, Theatre and Cinema Advertisements

If your ancestor was from a theatrical background you can trace their career through cast listings given in newspapers. Many will only name the lead actors in a play and the role they were playing may or may not be stated. If your ancestor is named, you should at least be able to discover what play they were in, where this was and the dates they were there. Where this was a large production you should be able to trace them as they toured around the country. For more local actors, provincial newspapers will often tell you the different roles they played in their local theatre. Specialist newspapers such as *The Stage* (from 1880 onwards) and *The Era* (1838–1939) are full of advertisements noting the location and latest role played by various performers.

Cinema listings can be of interest to family historians. There is obviously no guarantee that our ancestors watched any of the films that were advertised at the time they were alive, but it can still help to add context. If you speak to older relatives, you may be able to find out which films they watched at the cinema and find an advert for this to add colour to their timeline.

Performances of live music are common. Notable musicians and singers will be named and the name of an orchestra or choir. These can be useful search terms if you know your ancestor was a member. Large productions in cities will note if anyone of note is due to be in attendance, such as a member of the royal family or local MPs. Conductors are also usually named. Names are often given using surnames only, such as 'a solo on the oboe by Mr Cooke', so bear this is mind when deciding on a search term. You may find it is enough to search by the name 'Cooke' and the added keyword of 'oboe', depending on how common your ancestor's surname was.

Lost and Found

Another feature in the classifieds was the 'lost and found' section. This could feature a whole range of items from cookware to jewellery, and also featured pets. A notice in *The Hackney and Kingsland Gazette* on 5 October 1885 states: 'LOST – 5s Reward – On 22nd Sept., a black cat, with white paws and breast, and also on one side of nose, named Bobby. Apply 44 Graham Rd, Dalston.' If you search for articles via your ancestor's address you may find a result such as this. Whether they ever found Bobby or not will likely remain unknown, although sometimes a notice of thanks appears in later issues.

Some lost and found notices give a person's name (either the person who lost the item or found it) and sometimes other details, including their occupation, place of work or telephone number. These notices became more commonplace from the latter half of the nineteenth century before dwindling down to almost nothing today, whereby people tend to prefer

L O S T,
Between MARGATE and CHAPEL HILL,
On SUNDAY, September 7,
Between One and Two o'Clock,

A GOLD STOP WATCH,

With the Cypher of T O and a Stag's Head Creft on the Back
of the Cafe,
The Maker's Name THOMAS HILL, London;
A Steel Chain, three Gold Seals, and a Gold Key;
One of the Seals has the Cypher T O and a Stag's Head Creft,
the large one the Impreffion of Shipping, the other a Head.
Whoever has found the fame, and will bring it to BENSON's
HOTEL, or to Mr. WORSLEY, Sadler, fhall receive FIVE
GUINEAS Reward.
If offered to Sale flop it, and give Information as above,
and the fame Reward fhall be given.

An appeal for a lost watch in *The Kentish Gazette* on 13 September 1783 providing a description of the item, where and when it was lost and who to return it to. *(Content provided by the British Library Board. All rights reserved. With thanks to The British Newspaper Archive (www.britishnewspaperarchive.co.uk))*

to advertise lost and found items for free on social media. There are many very early examples, even dating back to the eighteenth century. These were not within a 'lost and found' column but were placed as notices in their own right among other advertisements and communications. They tend to refer to items of great value. An eighteenth-century example can be seen above regarding a mislaid watch.

Selling of Goods by Auction

As well as the auctions of houses and land, goods were advertised to be due for auction. This was often after a person died or retired and their unwanted household property and tools of their trade were to be sold. These notices are concise, giving the date, time and location of the auction and the items that are to be sold. They are usually found among auctions for land and property under a heading such as 'Sales by Auction' or similar. The name of the person selling is usually given, either in full or with a first initial, sometimes with their address. The reason for auction is sometimes given, such as a property move, retirement or death. The excerpt on the following page is a typical example of what you may find.

These auction notices are particularly helpful where the reason for selling is given. They can often help us to narrow down a date of

ON THURSDAY FIRST.

WITHIN WORKSHOP, No. 43 SCOURING-BURN, DUNDEE.

SALE, BY AUCTION, OF

BLACKSMITH'S STOCK-IN-TRADE & WORKING PLANT, ENGINE, BOILER, VERTICAL DRILLING MACHINE, IRON, &c.

(Belonging to Mr ANDREW WATSON, Jobbing Blacksmith, who is Retiring from Business),

COMPRISING:—

Horizontal Steam Engine, 4 Horse-Power; Egg-Ended Boiler, 10 ft. by 2 ft. 6 in., in Excellent Order: Valuable Vertical Drilling Machine, 1¾-inch Spindle, with Back Motion; Turning Lathe, 19 ft. Bed, with Counter Shaft, 9 inch Centre, all Complete: 2 Cast-Iron Forges, with Tops; 2 Pair Circular Bellows, 26 Inches; 4 Water Tea-Irons; 2 Anvils, by "WRIGHT;" Cast-Iron Anvil Blocks; 3 Vices, 6, 5½, and 5-inch Jaw; Screwing Taps and Dies, Assorted from ⅜ to 1¼ inch; Plumber's Pipe Cutters, Boring Rickets and Dices, Mandrills, Large Quantity Tongs and Bores, Grindstone and Trough, Fluted Rimblers, "SALTER'S" Spring Balance, Solder Pots, Lead, Quantity Bar Iron, Cast, Spindle, and Fallow Steel, Hammers, Blacksmith's Tools, Scrap, and other Effects.

Sale at 12 o'clock Noon.

JOHN C. CRABBE, Auctioneer, has been favoured with instructions to Sell as above.

No. 26 Commercial Street.

An advertisement for the auctioning of Andrew Watson's blacksmithing equipment due to his retirement, in *The Dundee Advertiser* on 22 August 1899. *(Content provided by the British Library Board. All rights reserved. With thanks to The British Newspaper Archive (www.britishnewspaperarchive.co.uk))*

death. If the reason given is retirement then you know the person is still alive although they may have recently become too unwell to work. If the reason is the person's death you know to search for a death before the date of publication. Where the reason given is a property move, the person's new home parish is unlikely to be provided. Huge quantities of livestock went through auctions, but the farms' or farmers' names are less commonly found than with other goods auctions. Similar notices can be found under headings such as 'To be Disposed of' and 'Sales by Contract'. These often feature similar information but are sold privately rather than through auction.

Legal Announcements

Numerous different types of legal announcements were placed in newspapers, sometimes appearing in their own column heading 'legal notices' or otherwise among the classifieds. These date back to the seventeenth century when they were originally placed in *The Gazette*. Many focus on debt. This may be if a person has recently died and their solicitor is requesting that anyone who owed them money pays this within a set number of days. This is a useful way of proving the death of an ancestor if no other evidence can be found, as you know they will have died prior to the date of the notice. There are also notices placed searching for relatives of recently deceased people where they died intestate. This tells you not only that a named person has recently died but also that they died without leaving a will.

Another common example is when a person placed an announcement stating that they will not be responsible for their spouse's debts after the date of the notice. Under the common law of coverture, a married woman's property was considered to belong to her husband. This also included any debts that she owed, which her husband would, therefore, be responsible for paying. Finding such a notice usually suggests that the couple have separated. The name of both the husband and wife will feature and usually their parish of residence. Such a notice was not always ironclad legally speaking; however, it would serve as a useful warning to local shopkeepers, tradesmen and creditors that the husband would not pay them for any goods his wife had purchased after that date.

If your ancestor changed their name, this may be publicised in the legal notices' column of their local newspaper, or in a national newspaper. The announcement will give their former full name and their new name, so whichever name you use as a search term, the relevant notice should appear. Using the date of the publication will help you to know which name you need to use to search for your ancestor in further newspaper

LEGAL NOTICE.

CHANGE OF NAME.—I, WILLIAM SMITH, of the Old Hall, Merton-road, Bootle, near Liverpool, and of Bankhall-street, Liverpool, contractor, hereby give notice that, by a Deed Poll dated the 16th day of February last, which said deed was on the 17th of the same month enrolled in the Chancery Division of the High Court of Justice, I have declared, and I do hereby declare, that I intend to prefix the name of ASTON to my name of WILLIAM SMITH, and that I intend henceforth to be called by the name of ASTON WILLIAM SMITH, and to use the said name of Aston William Smith in all deeds, documents, and writings, and for all purposes whatsoever. Dated this 12th day of March, 1880.

WILLIAM SMITH.

Witness: EDMUND PHIPPS, solicitor, Liverpool.   382

A legal notice placed by William Smith in *The Buxton Advertiser* on 20 March 1880 informing readers he has changed his name to Aston William Smith. *(Content provided by the British Library Board. All rights reserved. With thanks to The British Newspaper Archive (www.britishnewspaperarchive.co.uk))*

articles as well as other sources. Their place of residence and occupation is sometimes given. Unfortunately, the reason for the name change is not provided.

There are also numerous business announcements that appear in the legal notices' section of a newspaper, including new partnerships, the dissolution of existing partnerships, requests for applications for tenders and new contracts. The nature of the announcement will determine whether your ancestor appears by name or via their business's title. Notices of bankruptcy also appear in the column. Genealogical information is often supplied in business announcements, such as 'Thomas Stanbridge, son of the late Jeremiah Stanbridge of Aylesford, will continue the family masonry business in Black Street.'

Miscellaneous Advertisements

Multiple adverts were placed offering rewards for people who had absconded, including runaway children. There are numerous examples of employers trying to find runaway apprentices, such as in the *Sheffield Register* on 27 May 1791 where Master William Thackray, cordwainer of Wincobank offered a reward to find 18-year-old apprentice Thomas Petty. Thomas is described as 5 foot 4 inches tall, strongly built with sand-coloured hair. At the time he ran away, Thomas was wearing a dark green coat, a spotted velveret waistcoat and leather breeches. This paints a picture of Thomas in our minds; although why he felt the need to abscond we can only wonder. You may also come across adverts searching for runaway husbands and, particularly in America, runaway slaves. The latter were sometimes reprinted in national newspapers in Britain. Those who have absconded are described in detail, due to the lack of ability in early newspapers to print illustrations or photographs.

You will come across a wide range of other notices that do not quite fit into the categories above. All notices were a source of revenue for a newspaper so they were happy to accept anything as long as it was decent and relatively inoffensive. There are notices of gentlemen searching for men with capital to go into business with, people giving notice of their upcoming retirement, and tutors looking for private students.

Chapter 7

SPORT PAGES

We may find our ancestors mentioned in a newspaper if they were involved in sport. This may have been their occupation, such as a professional footballer, or simply taken up as a hobby. Often, finding them named this way is the first time we discover their love of a particular sport. It can be interesting to see how successful they were, where they played and read about any resulting injuries.

You may find your ancestor named if they were a sportsperson, a match official or a spectator who received an injury during play. Using newspaper articles, you can trace their sporting career and measure how their success changed with time. Scoring has changed for many sports so bear this in mind as they may have been more successful than you think. For example, if a team won four matches in a season they may have a higher percentage rate of wins compared with a team today who play more matches per season.

One issue that is more common when researching sporting ancestors is searching by name. In team sports, not all players will be named and where they are names are usually given using a first initial, such as 'J. Blundell'. This can make identification difficult, particularly if they only played a few matches. Players who made key contributions to a game may be named in a match write-up. Names may be spelt inaccurately in reports here as in other articles. This is often the case where sports journalists have heard a player's name but have not seen it written down. Bear this in mind when searching for spelling variations and think how they may be spelt phonetically.

If you do find that your ancestor partook in a game, it is worth researching its history. The rules of many sports have changed vastly over time with a massive improvement in health and safety regulations. This is not just for the players, but for spectators also who used to be allowed a lot nearer to the action, such as in motor racing and horse racing.

You may be interested to research what your ancestor would have worn while playing. Helmets were introduced relatively recently in many sports and other protective gear would also not have been worn in our ancestors' time. You may be surprised at what they would have dressed in. Of course, some lucky researchers will be able to see exactly what they wore if a photograph was printed in their local newspaper.

As with other events, if a sport was played on a major scale, such as a national tournament, you will find this in national newspapers as well as local newspapers. Most of our sporting ancestors, however, will only be found in their local newspaper or the newspaper that was local to the game. Remember to extend your search criteria to other counties when searching for a sporting ancestor, for this reason.

There have been several newspapers dedicated to sports news, such as *The Athletic News and Cyclists' Journal* (1875–1931) and *Sports Argus* (1897–2006). *The Illustrated Sporting and Dramatic News* (1874–1970) is an excellent newspaper containing a large number of photographs of sports events. This paper, and many others, initially focused on upper-class sports such as horse racing and hunting, but developed over time to include lacrosse, football, rugby and rowing, among many others.

Some people assume that only their male ancestors will appear in the sports pages, but there are numerous examples where women can be found. Ladies were permitted to play professional tennis at Wimbledon from 1884 onwards, with women also being found playing archery, golf and cricket from early on. *The Illustrated Sporting and Dramatic News* had multiple pages of each issue focused on women's achievements in a section titled 'The Sports Woman'.

The attitude towards women's sport is frequently reflected upon in newspapers. In *The Illustrated Sporting and Dramatic News* on 19 April 1902, it was remarked by an unnamed journalist:

Women golfers begin to get discontented at their treatment by some of the clubs. I always hoped that they would do this, as I had to give up belonging to two clubs because they debarred ladies from playing at practically the only times when I could have had a round. Insult was added to injury when a man friend told me that several men with handicaps lower than mine simply refused to let better players pass them, and were real nuisances, while the ladies, he was good enough to remark, were only imitation nuisances.

You may well discover, therefore, that a female sporting ancestor was a pioneer, breaking down boundaries for her sex in the sport.

As well as attitudes towards certain demographics of sport, you should also be aware of potential bias. Historically, some journalists reporting on sport would favour certain players or teams which would impinge on their write-up. If their favourite team lost a match, the report could be written in a way that made it sound unfair and that they did not deserve to lose. Unfortunately, even in sport reports we have to be conscious that they may not be entirely reliable and reflective of exactly what happened. Try researching reports on the same match from multiple newspapers. Even today, you will find match reports somewhat conflicting with each other in terms of the events that lead to the result, even if the final score is given correctly.

Evidence of an ancestor's love of sport may also appear in other sections of a newspaper. For example, you may find that they suffered an accident while cycling in a race against a friend or the theft of their tennis racket may appear in the courts' column. Even where your ancestor was simply playing a game with his family in a park or garden this is still of interest to know about their pastimes. The first evidence you come across of a person being involved in sport may be in their obituary, with a phrase such as 'well known in the rugby community'.

Historically, the first mentions of sport in newspapers only name the gentry and often focus around betting. In *The Caledonian Mercury* on 25 June 1728 it is noted that a cricket match is due to be played the following Tuesday near Maidstone by the Duke of Richmond and his club against Edward Steed Esq. and his club 'for a large sum'. Early reports only name the most well-known gentry of the time who were involved. In *The Kentish Weekly Post or the Canterbury News-Letter* on 25 April 1730 it is stated: 'Yesterday morning the Dukes of Devonshire and Richmond, the Earl of Albemarle, Lord James Cavendish and about 12 more, diverted themselves at cricket in Hyde Park and next week they are to play a match for 100 Guineas.' Starting odds for horse racing has remained a common fixture.

For the large majority of those named as being involved in sport, this will not have been their main occupation. It can sometimes be hard to know if they were paid at all. It can be confusing if you are tracing an ancestor who appears to play a sport professionally but they frequently give their occupation as something else in other records, such as census returns. Even where a person was paid, most will still have needed a reliable regular income from another occupation.

Initially, sporting news did not take up much space in newspapers, usually just a brief paragraph given here and there. As newspapers had such limited space, it may be that a Friday match report did not appear until the following Wednesday if that's when there was next space available. One of the first newspapers to dedicate an entire page to sports news was the *Weekly Dispatch* during the early nineteenth century. Much of this was focused on horse racing, boxing and cricket but others do feature. Sport reports increased towards the end of the nineteenth century and beginning of the twentieth century. With more column inches allowed for sporting news, you are more likely to find your ancestor named for sporting reasons from then on.

You may find sporting awards and trophies that were given to your ancestor, or records that they broke, even if this was only on a local scale. Discovering the speed at which your ancestor could run 100 metres can be of interest to compare with short-distance runners today. You could even pit yourself against them to see how you would fare! Any sporting medals or trophies may still be in the family, perhaps being cared for by a distant cousin, or you may find them within a museum, antique shop or online auction site.

Team Events

Where sporting ancestors played in a team they are less likely to be named. For many sports, such as cricket, the scores are often provided in full naming each player with their first initial and surname. In the accompanying write-up of the match, players may be named with their first name or only their surname if they did something noteworthy – such as score a goal or receive an injury.

Team events you may find your ancestor involved in include boat racing, football, rugby, cricket, hockey and curling – the latter particularly in Scotland. Once you have found evidence that your forebear was on a particular named team you can then use this team name as a search term to discover more. Where your ancestor's name is not given in an article or where OCR has not correctly transcribed their name, this team name is a useful term to use. In articles, team names are often given without naming individual players, so it can be difficult to determine if your ancestor was still involved or not.

It is worth remembering that much sporting documentation has survived outside of newspapers. You can search archives catalogues and some museum catalogues for your ancestor's name and their team name to see what they hold. This could include programmes, tickets, photographs, letters and objects such as bats and balls.

BOROUGH OF TYNEMOUTH CLUB.

1st Innings.		2nd Innings.	
J. Reed, b. J. Elliott	1	b. Shotton	0
J. Wheldon, b. Elliott	7	b. Elliott	4
C. Wheldon, b. Hart	0	not out	9
G. Wheldon, run out	4	c. Miller, b. Hart	2
W. Sutherland, b. Elliott	6	c. Miller, b. Elliott	3
R. Wheldon, c. Mather, b. Hart	7	b. Elliott	1
T. Crawford, c. Elliott, b. Elliott	4	b. Mather	5
H. Barker, b. Elliott	5	run out	1
W. Beall, run out	0	b. Shotton	3
R. Barker, b. Elliott	0	c. Elliott, b. Mather	0
W. Stobbs, not out	0	leg before wicket, b. Shotton	3
	34		31
Byes	3	Byes	1
Wides	2	Wides	2
		No balls	2
Total	39	Total	36

WESTOE CLUB.

1st Innings.		2nd Innings.	
G. S. Shotton, b, Reed	7	not out	7
G. Smith, leg before wicket, do.	0	not out	15
W. Hart, c. C. Wheldon, b. Reed	8		
E. Mather, b. R. Wheldon	10		
J. Elliott, b. R. Wheldon	3		
J. Jameson, b. Reed	1		
W. Cook, b. Reed	3		
L. Thomas, c. C. Wheldon b. Reed	1		
G. Miller, not out	2		
J. Clark, b. Reed	0		
C. Wawn, b. C. Wheldon	0		
	34		22
Byes	8	Byes	1
Wides	5	Wides	7
Total	47	Total	29

The cricket scores for Borough of Tynemouth Club v. Westoe Club in the *North & South Shields Gazette* on 7 September 1849. *(Content provided by the British Library Board. All rights reserved. With thanks to The British Newspaper Archive (www. britishnewspaperarchive.co.uk))*

Newspapers focused on sport and those local to the event are the most likely to name individuals in a team game. For example, the Oxford and Cambridge Universities boat race appears in the newspaper each year, with a build-up to the event as well as a report afterwards. Provincial newspapers outside of the area tend to give an overview of the race with few names given. Sporting papers and local papers to Oxford and Cambridge give much more detail. For example, in *The Oxford Times* on

8 April 1871 the rowers' names are given with first and middle initials along with their college and weight. Examples include H.J. Lomax of First Trinity College, Cambridge weighing 12st 2lbs and T.S. Baker of Queens College, Oxford weighing 13st 2lbs.

Cricket is a great sport to research as, where a scorecard is provided, each member's initial and surname is given with their number of runs; many other team events only name those who scored in a match, for example. This is true whether the cricket match was played officially or informally. The image on the previous page shows a typical example of this, with the first and second innings clearly shown. A long write-up precedes the scorecard; however, this only gives the first name of one player, Robert Wheldon of Tynemouth. It does, though, confirm the Wheldons are all brothers.

Individual Sportspeople

Where your ancestor played as an individual, it is often easier to trace their career as those playing sports as an individual are more likely to have a full name given. Players of golf, archery and tennis for example are frequently named and individual sports people are also often named in local newspapers. You may be able to trace the ups and downs of their sporting career this way. For example, if they were a cyclist, you may find that after a few years of being in the top three finishers they began to slip down the results table before disappearing altogether. You may also find evidence of a sporting injury that hampered their future results or ended their participation altogether.

There are obviously numerous exceptions. In horse racing, historically, the jockey was often not named at all as the name of the horse was seen as more important. In other sports, only nicknames or aliases are given. For example, in *The Scotsman* on 23 August 1823 it is noted that 'Fiery Burns' and 'Sloth Brown' fought in a boxing match for fifty minutes, consisting of eleven rounds. Their real names are not given, meaning you would need to know the men's nicknames to be able to research them in this way. It is worth noting that boxing was commonly known as pugilism so this is a good search term to use to trace a boxing ancestor.

There is a wide range of other individual sports that you may find your ancestor involved in, including fencing, tennis, cycling, billiards, athletics and badminton, among many others. Chess also appears regularly in sports columns, played individually or as a team, under named chess clubs. Any sport may be seen played as a team or a group. You may find your ancestor partook in cycling races as an individual but also took part of races as part of a local cycling club with a group result.

Sport participation often ran in families, initially through the higher classes who had access to facilities such as tennis courts, stables and swimming pools. You can find evidence of family relations in multiple sports columns. A player's parent may be named if they were previously involved in the sport, or siblings who play against each other. The image below is a report of the first female winner of Wimbledon, Maud Watson, detailing how she beat her sister who is named here only as 'Miss Watson'.

The final match for the Ladies' Championship, between Miss Watson and her sister, Miss Maud Watson, of the Cheltenham Lawn Tennis Club, produced some really brilliant play on the part of both ladies. The first set was won by Miss Watson by eight games to six. After some exciting play, at the end of which they were five games all, Miss Watson having won the first, fourth, sixth, seventh, and ninth games, Miss Maud won the advantage game. Then her sister equalised matters by taking the twelfth game. Miss Watson followed this up by winning the next two games in succession, and the set, as above stated. Throughout the whole 14 games deuce was called six times in game two, and twice in game six. The twelfth game, won by Miss Watson, was a love one. In the second set Miss Maud Watson carried off the first, second, third, fifth, eighth, and ninth games, and the set by six games to three. The eighth game was deuced twice, and the third and fifth games were love ones. The third set Miss Maud Watson won also by six games to three. Although Miss Watson did her best to avert defeat, Miss Maud won the first, second, sixth, seventh, eighth, and ninth games. The second game was deuced once, and games three and six were love games. Thus Miss Maud supplemented her victory in the Irish Ladies' Championship by winning the first Ladies' Championship of England by two sets to one. Miss Maud Watson can boast of a long and unbroken list of victories, as she has never yet been defeated in any single championship tournament.

A match report on the first Ladies Championship at Wimbledon between the two Watson sisters in London's *Evening Standard* on 21 July 1884. *(Content provided by the British Library Board. All rights reserved. With thanks to The British Newspaper Archive (www.britishnewspaperarchive.co.uk))*

Sporting Officials

Your ancestor may appear in the sport section of a newspaper, despite not playing themselves. This could be as a referee, coach, animal trainer, animal owner, linesman or sponsor for example. It is fairly common to find the names of trainers and owners to be named with regard to horse racing such as in the *Daily Express* on 31 May 1905 when it is recorded that a 2-year-old horse, 'Golden Measure', was owned by Mr J. Buchanan and trained by Major J.D. Edwards. If your ancestor is found acting as a referee or coach it is worth looking into whether they previously played the sport they are presiding over.

Umpires, referees and judges are often unfairly reported about. Their job involves making challenging decisions while maintaining fairness and following the rules of the sport; however, this is not always as clear cut as spectators would like it to be. Controversial decisions and mistakes made by sporting officials have been and remain the topic of many newspaper articles and correspondence to the publication. Alternatively, they may also be praised for upholding a sense of calm, order and fairness at a difficult time.

Spectators

Spectators are only named in newspapers if they were either members of the gentry or if they were injured. It was noteworthy to read about which members of royalty attended a horse race or if a duke attended a cricket match. Most ordinary members of the public will usually only be named if they were severely injured or killed while a spectator. The example on the following page is a sad case of how easily accidents happened due to the lack of health and safety regulations.

The size of the crowd at a particular sporting event is frequently noted, such as if tickets were sold out or that there was a record attendance. The demeanour of the crowd may also be featured, such as if they were particularly boisterous or overly quiet. Any other notable occurrences within the crowd may also be reported upon, such as violence and disorder among the spectators.

You may discover from family ephemera that has been passed down to you that your forebear supported a particular team or attended a particular match. You can again use newspapers to see what happened on that particular day, or how the team fared over the time your ancestor supported them. There is a very slim chance you may find a photograph of your ancestor as a spectator at a particular sporting event in the newspaper.

SERIOUS ACCIDENT AT FIRHILL FOOTBALL PARK.

BARRIERS GIVE WAY.

SPECTATORS INJURED.

A serious accident occurred at Firhill Park, Glasgow, the new ground of the Partick Thistle Football Club, during the progress of the Scottish League match between Partick Thistle and Celtic on Saturday afternoon. Just about ten minutes past three o'clock, after the game had been in progress for almost half an hour, Quinn, of the Celtic, scored the equalising goal of the first half, when, in their excitement, the crowd lurched forward, pressing the foremost spectators against the wooden barrier around the end of the field close to New City Road. This enormous pressure caused the barrier to give way, precipitating those immediately in front of it—mostly boys and young men—to the ground. This in turn accentuated the pressure of those behind, and the spectators nearest those who had fallen were pressed forward, and had perforce to trample upon the others, many being injured.

Among the injured are—

Michael Brady (a boy), 55 Murano Street—fracture of the left leg.

Thomas M'Millan, 792 Garscube Road—internal injuries.

Alexander Duncan (a boy), 68 Doncaster Street—right arm injured.

W. Wilson, 27 Kirkland Street—face bruises and internal injuries.

J. Orr, 17 Ferguson Street—broken thumb.

A sad report on injuries suffered by football spectators at Firhill Park in Glasgow in *Aberdeen Daily Journal* on 15 November 1909. Five of those involved are named along with their home address and details of their injury. *(with permission from DC Thomson & Co Ltd)*

Chapter 8

EDUCATION AND OCCUPATIONS

Much of our life is taken up by education and work and it was the same for our ancestors. We can discover a surprising amount about our ancestor's life at school and their resulting working life, whatever role they ended up in, through newspapers. In articles where your ancestor is named this will take you directly to an appropriate article. If they are not named, you will need to know the name of the school they attended and their workplaces. You may find this out from a newspaper, such as in an obituary, or it may be through another source such as school registers and occupational records held in a local archive. Once you have found out these details, you can then use their school, workplace and employer as search terms to see what was happening when your ancestor was there. Notable events, such as the rapid spreading of a contagious disease at school or a fire that burned down a mill, would likely have impacted on your ancestor.

There are numerous other events you may come across that may have happened while your ancestor was in education or work. One interesting example that crops up is a royal visit. Your ancestor is highly unlikely to be named in this, but if you are aware that they were attending at the time then they certainly would have known about it and may have been present for the visit. If they were a headmaster or workplace manager they are more likely to be named as the person who greeted their VIP. The example on the following page is typical of what you may find.

You may also discover what the conditions were like at a school or workplace. The buildings may have been subject to an investigation whose report was discussed in the local newspaper. This can help us to paint a picture of our ancestor's surroundings, such as if the school is described

---

ROYAL VISIT TO THE NEWPORT-MARKET INDUSTRIAL SCHOOL.

The Princess of Wales and the Grand Duchess Cesarevna, attended by the Countess Apraxine and the Hon. Mrs. Stonor, honoured the Newport-market Refuge and Industrial School with a visit yesterday morning. Their Imperial and Royal Highnesses were received on their arrival by Mr. Owen Morshead, the hon. secretary, and were conducted by him over the institution. After a cursory look at the refuge, which at this season of the year is almost entirely closed for inmates, the distinguished party spent upwards of an hour in the school, making a lengthened inspection of it in all the details of its arrangements. The boys, some 60 in number, were massed in one of the play-rooms, and their cheerful healthy appearance was sufficient of itself to excite their Royal Highnesses' warmest approbation. The dormitories, school-rooms, and workshops were next visited in turn, and both the Princess and the Grand Duchess repeatedly expressed to Mr. Morshead their unqualified admiration, not only of the special objects of interest to be found in each of them, but at the general cleanliness, order, and method which pervade the establishment.

The Hon. Colonel Wood, Captain Pearse, R.N., and other members of the committee were present on the occasion, which will long be remembered as a red-letter day in the annals of the institution.

A report on the royal visit to Newport-Market Industrial School as seen in London's *Evening Standard* on 22 July 1873. *(Content provided by the British Library Board. All rights reserved. With thanks to The British Newspaper Archive (www. britishnewspaperarchive.co.uk))*

as unsanitary or a factory is designated as dilapidated. Alternatively, the report may give a report of the layout of a notable building to our ancestor's education or working life. Even reports stating how many children attended a school or how many people worked for a named employer can help us understand more about their day-to-day life. Where photographs or illustrations are included these are of more use.

There are often reports of sickness in named education settings and workplaces. A report in the *Tamworth Herald* on 14 April 1888 stated: 'the last term at Eton has been described as sickness term' with over 140 pupils absent due to illness and as a result there were 'several deaths'. If your ancestor died of a contagious disease you may find similar reports to explain where they may have caught it. If you are uncertain about an ancestor's cause of death then such an article may hint towards a possible cause. If the article is dated prior to the introduction of civil registration on 1 July 1837 then this is of more interest, as a death certificate is not available.

School News

Schools have always appeared in local newspapers. Providing school news and updates and naming as many children as possible are a great money-maker for newspapers, with eager parents keen to keep a copy of an issue with their child's name inside. Some school news will appear in other columns, which are mentioned in other chapters, such as accidents. Schools also frequently featured in court columns, with parents fined for their child's non-attendance. An example of this can be seen below.

It was common for parents to intentionally keep children home from school. When compulsory education was introduced, this was a huge shift for large families who previously had older children with them to help with childcare of younger siblings or to assist their father in the family business. At times, articles will give a parent's reasoning for their child's absence from school. This may be an innocent matter, such as a child suffering from a chronic illness. The reason may also give genealogical information, such as the severe illness, disability or death of a parent or sibling.

SCHOOL ATTENDANCE.

Parents were fined as follows for the irregular attendance of their children at school:— William Seymour, of Hooe, 2s. 6d. each, in respect of two children; John Attwood, Bexhill, 1s.; George Freeman, Bexhill, 1s.; William Sands, Dallington, 3s.; Thomas Hayler, Crowhurst, 1s. 6d.; John Pilbeam, of Hooe, was summoned for employing William Midmore, aged 12 years, contrary to the Education Act, and was fined 2s. 6d. and costs.

A list of parents fined at petty sessions for their children's irregular school attendance in the *Bexhill-On-Sea Observer* on 16 July 1898. Note that only parents are named, with the exception of the last case where a boy had been working at 12 years old. (*Content provided by the British Library Board. All rights reserved. With thanks to The British Newspaper Archive (www. britishnewspaperarchive.co.uk)*)

At other times, children were absent from school due to truancy, without their parent's knowledge. In the *Canterbury Journal* on 14 June 1913 it was reported:

> The St Augustine's Bench of Magistrates at Canterbury on Saturday made an order that George Saunders, the son of William Saunders, should attend school regularly, the lad who is 13 years of age, only having made 7 attendances out of a possible 39 ... Defendant said he only had a housekeeper, and the lad would not obey her and he could not stay away from work to see that the boy attended school.

You may find evidence that your ancestor attended a truant school. Examples of these include the Midland Truant School in Lichfield and the North London Truant School. The reports into the conditions here can be a window into your ancestor's quality of life. The example on the following page, regarding the truant school at Merthyr Tydfil in Wales, highlights this.

There are many other types of school you may find your ancestor attending. An article in the *Western Daily Mercury* on 21 November 1895 reported:

> A special application to fine Mr Henry Snow for not sending his son Reginald, a deaf mute, to a deaf-mute school was made. Mr Cook explained that the Board had gone to some expense in establishing a deaf and dumb school ... The head mistress had explained to the father that she hoped not only to be able to recover the boy's power of speech, but to enable him to lip-read ... This education was not appreciated in the least by the father and he therefore made an application for the maximum fine to be inflicted.

Other schools include industrial schools and boarding schools. You may be interested to read articles about when the schools were set up, how the location of them was decided upon and who funded their creation. Equally, you may wish to research articles about when schools were closed down and what the buildings were transformed into, if they are still standing today.

There are many positive aspects to researching an ancestor's school education. The most obvious is where they are named for having received an award or passed a particular course. In both cases, your

THE TRUANT SCHOOL.

The following report from Dr. W. W. Jones, of Merthyr, the medical officer of the school, was read to the committee at their ordinary meeting on Thursday, and the secretary instructed to send copies of same to each of the Association Boards, viz.:—Gentlemen,—I have the honour to submit to you my first annual report.

Sites and Buildings.—The sites and buildings have proved themselves admirably adapted for the purposes for which they are intended. The system of warming and ventilation has been at all times quite satisfactory. At the commencement of the year some of the walls were found to be very damp, but that has now been remedied, and you now have a building thoroughly dry and satisfactory in all respects.

Drainage.—Some difficulty has arisen during the year in regard to the disposal of refuse water and other sewage matter, and a number of cases of diarrhœa, during the hot weather of July, caused me a little anxiety, but I am glad to learn that there is now a prospect of an early settlement of the question by connecting the school with the main sewer. When that is done a proper disconnecting chamber should be made, and the drainage system will then be entirely satisfactory.

Inmates.—198 boys have been admitted during the year, the average age at time of admission being nearly 11 years. All the boys are brought under my notice after admission, and are again examined on being licensed out ; the great majority of them present a most neglected appearance, some of them indeed looking half-starved, but during their residence all of them show a marked improvement, not only physically, but also in intelligence. I have vaccinated any boys who on admission have been found to have been previously unvaccinated.

An extract from a report of the medical officer of the truant school at Merthyr Tydfil seen in *The Merthyr Times* on 7 February 1895, detailing the state of the building, as well as the pupils' condition. *(Content provided by the British Library Board. All rights reserved. With thanks to The British Newspaper Archive (www. britishnewspaperarchive.co.uk))*

ABERDEEN GIRL'S SCHOOL RECORD.

Aberdeen has secured the distinction of what is believed to be a British record for regular attendance at school. For 13½ years Miss Isabella Peters, 3 Osborne Place, a scholar at the Central Higher Grade School, has attended her classes daily without a single break in that long period, and at a meeting of the Attendance Committee of the School Board her achievement was commented on by the members. It was agreed to present her with a prize for her record.

A notice that Isabella Peters was awarded for 13½ years of regular attendance whilst a pupil at Central Higher Grade School in Aberdeen as seen in *Dundee Evening Telegraph* on 16 September 1913. (*Content provided by the British Library Board. All rights reserved. With thanks to The British Newspaper Archive (www. britishnewspaperarchive.co.uk)*)

ancestor will be named along with their achievement. As with other articles, their name may be given in full or using first and middle initials.

The example above is particularly helpful to us as researchers as the pupil's full name is given along with her home address. Not all articles are as helpful. A more common type of article can be seen in the *Tottenham and Edmonton Weekly Herald* on 23 August 1889 which gives the names of the boys at the top of their class in each subject at Latymer School as follows: 'History – 1st class, Rhymer; 2nd, Kingston; 3rd, Hoyle; 4th, Heath'. If you know that your ancestor was the only person by that surname to have attended that class then you can be fairly sure this article refers to them; however, that would need a thorough reading of their school registers and log books.

Examples such as that above are especially hard to find. If your ancestor was the boy named Heath who was fourth in class a surname search simply for Heath brings up nearly 13 million results, at the time of writing. Narrowing this down by adding the name of their school of 'Latymer' gives us just over 3,500 results. By filtering the date to 1889 when Heath was known to be a student reduces the results to 64; a much more manageable number to read through.

Graduating classes may be named, especially so in more recent times. This is largely again a business technique to try to encourage a boost in sales from proud parents who wish to keep a copy of their child's name in the newspaper. Those who partook in school plays are often named with the character they played, sometimes with a photograph. Likewise, if they were in the school choir they may also appear.

When researching your ancestor's school life, newspapers are excellent for reminding us of the challenging conditions faced by students. One such aspect regards physical discipline from teachers. There are many articles of court cases where teachers were questioned as to whether the form of discipline they used was too extreme. In an article in the *Lincolnshire Echo* on 2 March 1894, teacher Elizabeth Morriss was questioned regarding the apparent assault of 12-year-old student Florence Creasey at Bracebridge School in Lincoln. After Florence failed to correctly create a buttonhole in a garment, Miss Morriss was accused of hitting her with a closed fist 'four or five times'. Multiple pupil witnesses attested to this fact and a policeman confirmed the girl was bruised on her back as a result. Despite this, two teachers who witnessed the event stated that they 'did not think the punishment was excessive' and the Bench decided to dismiss the case. Miss Morriss escaped with only a verbal warning. There are many shocking reads such as this, which today would undoubtedly result in the teacher losing their job. It is worth reading about any such cases that arise from your ancestor's school, to give you an idea of what punishment was seen to be acceptable there at the time.

There is very little evidence in newspapers regarding inappropriate student-teacher relationships. It is frequently mentioned that teachers have been dismissed and dealt with by the Education Board; however, schools were usually able to keep details about these matters away from the press. Today a student-teacher relationship often makes the national news as well as local news. In the past it was kept quiet.

School sporting events are popular articles. Teams travelled across the local area to play rival schools. Reports of these games feature in local newspapers although usually only the surnames of key players are given, such as a cricketer who got the most runs or a footballer who scored the most goals. If you know from other records that your ancestor was part of a school team you can still track their progress through the newspapers even if they are named by using the school and sport as search terms, such as 'Enderby Boys' and 'cricket'.

Sunday schools were established in Britain in the eighteenth century and also appear in newspapers. Articles may name organisers, describe related events and name pupils, although the latter is less common than with educational schools. The example on the following page is a less common case where several of the pupils are named as having sung a solo at a service.

Church Sunday School. — Sunday School anniversary services were held in the Parish Church on Sunday, when the Vicar (Rev. A. Edgar) conducted special services in the afternoon and evening. Excellent congregations were present and were addressed by the Vicar, who also spoke to the children. Special singing was rendered by the children and choir, and solos were contributed to by the following scholars: Edna Ward, Marjorie Broddle, Bernard Broddle, Alice McGill, Marjorie Grantham, Vera Atkinson, Biddy Wilson, Becky Harness, Gwen Doe, Betty West, Maisie Clayton, Phyllis Libell and Kenneth Campion. Heartiest congratulations are extended to Miss F. Smith, who so capably presided at the organ throughout and was responsible for the excellent presentation by the children.

A report on North Somercotes Sunday School services naming many pupils and one member of staff in the *Louth and North Lincolnshire Advertiser* on 8 August 1936. *(Content provided by the British Library Board. All rights reserved. With thanks to The British Newspaper Archive (www.britishnewspaperarchive.co.uk))*

As well as researching students of a school, the above will also of course be of interest to those researching teaching ancestors. Teachers may be named as being appointed, being dismissed or retiring as well as more minor events, such as judging sports days and taking part in a fundraiser.

University and Adult Education

The age of compulsory education has changed several times since the late nineteenth century. Elementary education was made compulsory for children aged 5–10 in 1880. The leaving age increased to 11 in 1893, 12 in 1899, 14 in 1918, 15 in 1947 and 16 in 1972.

There are articles naming my grandfather Robert Samuel Eggelton as having completed a technical course in 1935 and a typing course in 1936 at Bletchley Evening Institute. Knowing he was aged 15 and 16 at the time I can tell he was not there because he legally had to be in education. As with so many genealogical facts, we cannot know whether my grandad chose the courses himself or how much influence his parents or previous teachers had on the decision to extend his time studying.

Graduating university classes are again frequently named as they are with school classes. The title of a student's thesis may be given, giving a real insight into their studies and specific interest. One example is seen in *St Andrews Citizen* on 17 October 1925 where student William Stewart Duke Elder graduated with an MD degree from the University of St Andrews with his thesis entitled 'Reaction of the eye to changes in the Osmotic pressure of the blood'.

University sports teams are reported on in a similar way to school sports teams albeit with a slightly more competitive feel. In particular, the annual boat race of Oxford and Cambridge Universities can make for interesting reading. The results of matches are given, with important players named, along with other facts, such as any notable people attending, any injuries that occurred, and the weather conditions.

There are reports on societies and clubs at universities, including election of student members, particular debates that occurred and dates of meetings. Students may also be named if they took part in a protest if this was deemed newsworthy enough. Pupils are also listed frequently with regard to prize-givings, including monetary awards, as well as scholarships and fellowships.

Adult education has hugely increased in the twenty-first century but the concept is not new. Adult schools began to appear in the eighteenth century and Mechanics' Institutes emerged in the early nineteenth century. The Workers' Educational Association (WEA) was also founded at the beginning of the twentieth century. You may find evidence of your ancestor attending one of these institutions.

Occupations

No matter what your ancestor's occupation was, you will be able to find out more about it through reading historical newspapers. Some examples of what you may find are business advertising as seen in the Advertising chapter and accidents at work as seen in the Accidents and Natural Disasters chapter of this book.

Some occupations feature more in newspapers. Policemen, lawyers and Justices of the Peace feature frequently in court reports. Medical professionals are often quoted in coroners' inquests, court reports and with regard to public health matters. Politicians will feature heavily as well as those of a high military standing.

Members of the clergy feature more than most with regard to their occupation. Their appointment to a new parish or ordination may be noted, as well as any fundraising efforts. Noteworthy sermons may be reported on, particularly if they were about a current news topic. Clergy may be named in disciplinary matters and are more likely to have an obituary published in their local newspaper.

It is possible to discover much about publicans. My great great-grandfather Charles William Bowler was a publican, first of the Fox and Hounds in Heath and Reach in Bedfordshire in 1881–1889 and then a lengthier stay at The Bull and Butcher in Fenny Stratford in Buckinghamshire from 1889 to around 1920. He features in multiple newspaper reports, including hosting meetings of the local angling association, the Band of Hope Lodge friendly society and harvest dinners. It is also noted that he had potatoes stolen from his land and on a separate occasion he was rewarded for helping to catch a criminal who was staying in the pub. You also may find publicans fined for irresponsibly serving drinks to men who are already deemed to be much under the influence of alcohol. Notes of changes in licence can also be found, such as in *The Bucks Advertiser and Aylesbury News* on 7 September 1889 when the licence for Fox and Hounds transferred from Charles Bowler to David Giltrow. Once you know the name of the pub where your ancestor worked, you can use this as a search term to read about noteworthy events from their time there.

You may think that you are unlikely to come across your agricultural labourer ancestors in newspapers with articles related to their work; however, you may be surprised. Evidence of agricultural competitions can be found in newspapers from the late eighteenth century. Prizes were awarded to winners of various categories, such as ploughing and sheep shearing. My great great-grandfather Walter Eli Hatcher appeared in the *Southern Times and Dorset County Herald* on 24 March 1900 having come second in a hedging competition at Winterborne Came. The top three from each class are named in full along with their parish; in Walter's case this is Bincombe. Newspapers can also be used to track farming prices, crop failures and the introduction of new farming technology. There are also frequent reports of livestock sales and agricultural hiring fairs in local newspapers.

Your ancestor may have been involved in an industrial strike. This most famously occurred in multiple mining strikes, such as the 1926 General Strike, due to increasing working hours and pay cuts. Depending on whether the strike was national, such as this was, or not, may depend on whether you can assume your ancestor took part in it. Sometimes a specific colliery may be named, whereas at other times newspapers simply report on miners' strikes within a named county, such as Yorkshire or Staffordshire.

Upon retirement, or sometimes after a work 'anniversary', such as being employed in the same company for twenty-five years, testimonials are often found in newspapers. These often surround a presentation dinner or similar event which can provide a short biography. Much will be focused on their occupational history, including their educational background, but familial information is also often provided, particularly if any family members have previously been or are currently involved in the same industry. These are usually very positive features, with any negative aspects of the person's character or history often overlooked.

There are a number of newspapers which are aimed at specific occupations. These include *The Agricultural Advertiser and Tenant-Farmers' Advocate* and *The Stage*. If such a newspaper exists for your ancestor these will be worth reading to see what topics were important to the industry in their period.

In more general terms, you can read articles about occupations as they began to dwindle in popularity, largely due to the ever-changing improvement of technology. Many of the occupations that our ancestors had have decreased massively over time, such as wheelwrights and chimney sweeps. Others have been made obsolete, such as lamplighters. It can be of interest to read how these changes were reported in the press and perhaps link it to a change in occupation for your own ancestor. For example, if they worked as a rope-maker in 1861 but by 1871 they were working as an agricultural labourer you may want to research if the rope-making industry was in decline at the time. The attitude towards this decline can hint at the contemporary public feelings. Perhaps it was viewed with great optimism of cheaper products and faster labour or perhaps there was sadness or anxiety about the winding down of traditional work.

One such example can be seen in the *Western Mail and South Wales News* on 25 February 1932. In an article titled 'Saving the Smithy' the decline of the blacksmith industry in Monmouthshire is discussed. A survey is examined which found that 30 per cent of blacksmith yards were closed and 50 per cent only made a very small profit described as 'a mere pittance'. Only 20 per cent were described as working 'fitfully'. It is admitted that the blacksmiths 'cannot hope to compete with modern technology, so they confine their craft to the forging of articles that can be worked only in the smithy'.

There are plenty of articles which describe the typical day in the life of a person in a named occupation. While we may not know the exact hours or conditions our ancestor worked within, reading about those who worked in the same role can give us a good idea of what daily life was like for them and what problems they may have faced. There are often differences in roles between counties so when researching particular jobs, try and find an article from as close to your ancestor's location as possible.

Newspapers are especially useful for discovering more about obsolete occupations. One of the best examples is the role of a 'knocker-up' whose job it was to tap on the windows of working people to ensure they were awake and ready for work themselves. This was an important role in a time before reliable alarm clocks. In *The Leeds Times* on 17 November 1877 there is a fantastic article about a lady named only as Mrs Waters who worked as a knocker-up for thirty-five years. The article goes into great detail about what the role involved, how it changed over time and describes her favourite and least favourite customers. The below is an excerpt from the article but if your ancestor was a knocker-up it is advised you read the whole article. Whatever occupation your ancestor was in, try searching for similar articles from the time to give you an idea of what their lives involved.

"The reason why knocking-up is so widespread now-a-days is this ; people soon get so used to the alarum-clock that it fails to awake them, or if it awake them, they are at times so sleepy that they drop off again before the alarum runs out. This was the case with the person who asked me to awaken him. Well, I engaged with him ; and a good thing it was for me, for before a year had gone over my head I had thirty customers of the like kind. No ; not for the same hour in the morning, nor for the like pay—begging your pardon—but mostly for the time between five and six o'clock. I have no objection whatever to tell you what I used to earn ; why should I? But let me tell you first how I went on adding to my business, if I may call it a business. At the end of the first year, as I have said, I had thirty customers. Year by year they went on increasing, until at the end of five years I had near eighty houses to go to ; and for the thirty years that I followed knocking-up after that—thirty-five in all—I never fell below that number. Sometimes I had as many as ninety-five. What did they pay? All prices. When I got a few more early customers in addition to my first one, I knocked him a shilling a week off ; for I could not fashion to take half a crown. So all who were knocked up before four o'clock paid me eighteenpence a week ; whilst those who had to be awakened soon after four gave me a shilling a week ; while those who had to be aroused from five to six o'clock paid from sixpence to threepence weekly, according to time and distance. Of course the greater number of customers belonged to the threepeny class."

An extract from the fascinating article about Mrs Waters, a knocker-up, as seen in *The Leeds Times* on 17 November 1877. (*Content provided by the British Library Board. All rights reserved. With thanks to The British Newspaper Archive (www. britishnewspaperarchive.co.uk)*)

Chapter 9

TRAVEL AND SHIPPING NEWS

Your ancestor may have travelled overseas, in land on rail or worked at sea. If so, newspapers are a fantastic source of information to track them down. This could be through searching them by their name, the name of the ship they travelled on, the name of the ship they worked on or via an emigration scheme. Shipping is closely linked to the weather so searching weather reports can add to your understanding of their journey.

The constant improvements to travel have always been interesting to readers. Newspapers have overseen the introduction of motor vehicles, massive improvements to the durability, safety and speed of ships and the initiation of the railways. We can use newspapers to track changes to the infrastructure near our ancestor's parish, including the building of canals, railways and roads. If they worked in the industry such as a railway stationmaster or a dockworker, articles about new railway stations or the hiring of new employees will be of interest.

Travel often resulted in accidents, whether at sea, by rail or otherwise. These were newsworthy topics covered by local and national press, often with names of people who died and the names of crew members or drivers found to be at fault. Inquests go into great detail about these types of incidents with several witnesses quoted as to what they say happened on the day. More can be read about this in the Accidents and Incidents chapter of this book.

Historically, people travelled abroad for the same reasons as we do today. This may be a permanent move where a person or family emigrated to another country. It could also be a temporary trip, such as to study, work abroad or visit relatives. If a family experienced a birth, marriage or death while abroad, these notices were frequently sent to the provincial newspaper nearest to their previous residence in their home country. This was often seen as the best way to notify a number of friends and relatives of their news in one go, in a time before telephones and the internet.

Newspapers will all feature news regarding travel and shipping in some form. There are more specialised newspapers, such as *Lloyd's List* which was established in 1726 and subtitled 'the leading daily shipping newspaper', and the *Shipping and Mercantile Gazette* published 1838–1884. These are both fantastic newspapers in which to trace the comings and goings of ships around the world. Many newspapers copied their shipping news directly from *Lloyd's List* so you may find the same information repeated multiple times in several different titles. If you do find your ancestor travelling abroad, remember to track the overseas newspapers from their destination country in case they featured in them while they were there.

Passenger Lists and Travel Announcements

Newspapers sometimes published passenger lists of those who were arriving into the country or departing from it. This is more common if the newspaper was based in a county bordering the sea with a port, such as Liverpool or Southampton. In case of smaller ships, you may find every passenger is named; however, in most cases only the wealthier classes are noted. People such as royalty, aristocracy, politicians, businessmen and opera singers were frequently listed with regard to their movements. These passenger lists may only give their names but can also provide other details, including their ages, occupations and final destinations. The name of the ship and the country they are departing from will also be given.

Sometimes genealogical information is provided with regard to relationships between passengers. In the *Daily Express* on 12 August 1914 an 'almost complete' passenger list of the *A. P. Bernstorff* steamship was printed. This extremely lengthy list gives relationships but no names other than the lead traveller, such as 'Fred Breymayer, wife and three children', and 'Mrs Whitley, son and daughter'. Each family's home town is also provided to help with identification. The format of each passenger list varies between newspaper titles with different amounts of detail provided in each.

Only a few passenger lists were printed in newspapers. However, if you discover the surviving passenger list elsewhere, you can then use the name of the ship and the dates they travelled to discover more about their journey. Details often include the number of crew and the number of passengers on-board in each class. The example below states that a

PASSENGERS FOR NEW YORK.

The steamer *New York* left Southampton on Saturday last with about 200 saloon passengers, 200 second cabin, and upwards of 400 steerage. Among the passengers were several persons from the Channel Islands on their way to the Chicago Exhibition.

A report on the ship New York leaving Southampton, from the *Jersey Express* dated 9 May 1893. *(Content provided by the British Library Board. All rights reserved. With thanks to The British Newspaper Archive (www.britishnewspaperarchive.co.uk))*

number of passengers were travelling to see the Chicago exhibition in New York, a fact that you would not be able to fathom from a passenger list alone.

Travel announcements also included the arrival of notable people to named hotels. This can help you trace ancestors after they landed in the country or during their domestic travels within the country. An announcement in *The Western Times* on 4 March 1884 simply states: 'Mr and Mrs Lothian Bell have arrived at the Pulteney Hotel from Torquay.' These announcements will also be relevant to readers whose ancestors owned or worked in the hotel at the time. The upper classes are frequently named as having arrived in London, having departed to their estate elsewhere or as attending a named social event. This became less frequent in the twentieth century and today the public are more inclined to read about the movements of celebrities rather than the upper classes.

You can find dedicated columns to such people's whereabouts in many newspapers. In *The New Times* on 17 March 1823 an example of their 'Fashionable Mirror' column can be seen, divided into 'Fashionable Parties' and 'Fashionable Movements'. People are named with their titles, such as Lord King, the Marchioness of Salisbury and Earl Morley, along with either the party or dinner they held or the locations they travelled between. Some are specific naming hotels and streets, whereas others are much more vague, such as, 'the Earl of Clare has left town on a tour.' Underneath is a list of health updates of the upper classes, both those who are unwell and those who have recovered from a previously reported illness. These often give the person's location, such as, 'Viscountess Bulkeley, we regret to state, is quite indisposed, at her house in Stanhope Street, Mayfair.'

Emigration Schemes

Emigration has, at times in history, been encouraged, and at other times forced upon members of the public. Various schemes were devised to entice people to other countries, with newspapers being used as a way of advertising to prospective travellers. You may find quotes and letters from previous migrants published in newspapers, informing the readers of how successful they have been overseas and how happy they are in their new country. Other articles offer advice to potential future emigrants. Newspapers informed readers how and where tickets could be purchased and informed readers of mass movements of emigrants.

BARNADO BOYS FOR CANADA.

ON Thursday morning the 204th party of immigrants from Dr. Barnardo's homes left for Canada, sailing from Liverpool by the steamship Tunisian (Allan Line). The party consisted of 380 young people (292 boys and 88 girls). All the boys and girls who are old enough will be, on landing, at once placed in situations already chosen for them, and the younger children will be boarded out in Canadian households. Including this party the homes have now sent out 22,017 boys and girls, of whom all but an insignificant minority of under 2 per cent. have done well. Many previous emigrants now own their own farms.

A report stating that the ship *Tunisian* had left Liverpool for Canada with 380 children as part of the Barnardo's emigration scheme from *The Illustrated Police News* dated 19 March 1910. *(Content provided by the British Library Board. All rights reserved. With thanks to The British Newspaper Archive (www.britishnewspaperarchive. co.uk))*

The emigrants themselves are rarely named, but you can trace named ships. The article on the previous page regards the famed Barnardo's emigration scheme of children to Canada.

Reports about Travel Conditions

If you know the name of the ship on which your ancestor travelled, you may discover an article about the conditions on-board. As you would expect, to make the news the conditions either had to be luxurious or particularly dangerous or unsanitary – and it was usually the latter. Articles about ships where multiple passengers and crew were struck down by a contagious illness can make for uncomfortable reading but will be eye-opening to those related to somebody on-board.

It can be hard to imagine what it was like for our ancestors travelling abroad by ship. Conditions were variable and many were very cramped and tickets oversold. Newspapers can really bring their journey to light and help us to understand what passengers went through and the sights that they would have seen. There are stories of food running out, pest infestations, calamitous weather, illness and death on-board. There are also articles about fighting and assaults which happen on-board, somewhat inevitable with so many people cramped in a small space for a long time.

Numerous articles exist with interviews from passengers. In the *Liverpool Albion* on 12 November 1838, one passenger named only as Mr Bennett described his journey on-board *The Royal William*: 'In a day, or a day and a half, two-thirds of the passengers were sea-sick. What a horrible, pleasant, execrable, delightful, singular, excruciating sensation sea-sickness is!. … The ladies, poor souls, suffered awfully.' Conversely, there are also positive stories. In the *Liverpool Weekly Courier* on 28 September 1872 a passenger from the ship *Austrian* stated:

> All the passengers were made to be quiet and orderly; after eleven at night the lights were put out and silence reigned. I slept comfortably in my berth, quite as well as I have ever done on board ship. The officers of the ship were well behaved, gentlemanly men and the strictest discipline was maintained.

Naturally, you will find negative stories of conditions feature more heavily as this is of more interest to the reader.

The article on the following page details an emigrant's complaints about his journey from Glasgow to Queensland. A search for the ship name would bring up this search result.

THE SUFFERINGS OF STEERAGE PASSENGERS.

SERIOUS CHARGES AGAINST GLASGOW SHIPOWNERS.

A Bradford emigrant who sailed in the s.s. Duke of Argyll, which left Glasgow on the 29th of November last for Queensland, has sent to the Agent-General in London a memorial signed by 247 passengers, complaining of the treatment they received. The memorialists first of all complain of the wretched manner in which they were lodged at the Standard Hotel, Glasgow, where they had to remain for six days, huddled together in filth and dirt, with insufficient food, and treated more like pigs than human beings. After complaining of the want of washing and sleeping accommodation on board ship, the memorialists say that for four weeks the bread was so sour and bitter that it was with the greatest difficulty any portion of it could be eaten. The rice and porridge were burned in the cooking, and given in such scanty measure that often four persons did not get more than a pint between them. The beef, pork, or potted meat were generally thrown overboard as they were being fetched from the cooking galley, most of them being unfit for human food. Other complaints relate to the extortionate prices charged for eatables which the passengers were obliged to obtain at the ports of call owing to the shipping company not supplying sufficient food: the price charged by the steward for ginger ale and lemonade—viz., sixpence per bottle, and for beer one shilling per bottle; and the drudgery of five hours' work each day in the broiling sun, to which the messmen were subjected, and for which they received nothing. Most of the emigrants, who on starting were strong and healthy, are now thin, weak, and sad. The supply of limejuice was stopped on Wednesday, January 9th, four days before arriving at Batavia, causing much suffering from thirst, as the water supplied was on many occasions nearly boiling. In conclusion, it is complained that the convenience for cooking was quite inadequate for the number of people. The following is the size of the only emigrants' cooking galley :— 14 feet by 10 feet, and 7 feet in height. In this two cooks and two assistant cooks had to prepare the food of 500 people.

The complaints of an unnamed man travelling from Glasgow to Queensland on the SS *Duke of Argyll,* giving a real insight to the conditions faced by passengers and crew in *The Dundee Courier & Argus* on 25 March 1884. *(Content provided by the British Library Board. All rights reserved. With thanks to The British Newspaper Archive (www.britishnewspaperarchive.co.uk))*

Shipping News

The shipping news column was present in many newspapers in the eighteenth century but reached its peak in the nineteenth century. This declined in the twentieth century. The column will be of use to you if you have seafaring ancestors such as captains of ships, cabin crew, fishermen and dockworkers. Most of the column is made up of the incoming and outgoing ships to named ports. Outside of wartime, the column could also be used to track ships belonging to the Royal Navy, including ship launches.

At its peak, the shipping news column often took up several pages of a newspaper. Advertisements appeared here regarding boats for sale, tickets for upcoming voyages, and itineraries for boating day trippers. This even included boat trips on inland lakes so may have been of use to your ancestors even if they never left their landlocked county. On the other hand, there are also early reports of worldwide explorations and the European discoveries of 'new' islands.

It is, of course, the ship arrivals and departures that are likely to be of most use to many researchers. The maritime industry was massive and you can use the column to trace the movements of ships on which your ancestor served, whether they were a captain, navy rating or otherwise. You may be aware, from another source, that your ancestor was a captain of a ship and be able to use newspapers to discover the name of the ships that they served on. Be careful, however, as often only surnames are given. You may discover a Captain Frampton leaving Poole Harbour and assume it is your ancestor, being unaware there was another man of the same name with the same occupation. As with any source, you can use newspapers to then prove or disprove the information from another record.

Detail in shipping columns was sometimes kept very brief. For example, in the *Shields Daily Gazette* on 31 March 1892 updates were kept short, such as 'Serica, Bombay for Hull, left Ferrol on the 26th', with no further details. You would therefore need to know the ship name as *Serica*; however, once this is known you can then track her movements via the shipping news. Again, be careful; ship names were notoriously used more than once. Be sure to use other sources and further articles to confirm you are tracing the right ship. Keep a close eye on the reported dates as well. In early newspapers, the news of a ship's arrival in a foreign country could take a long time to reach the British press, sometimes several months.

Interesting details, along with the captain's name, would often include the company that the ship belonged to and the nature of the cargo being transported, such as textiles, tea and livestock. Mail ships, sometimes recorded as postal steamers, were also kept track of. In fact, some newspapers columns were jointly entitled 'Mail and Shipping News', since the two were entwined.

Relevant weather and tidal information was also found in shipping news columns, including the cycle of the moon, times of high tide and the wind direction. Any navigational hazards were noted, as well as accidents, even if they did not result in any injuries or fatalities. In the *Shipping and Mercantile Gazette* on 5 March 1874, a long list of such boats appears under their usual column heading of 'Wrecks and Casualties'. This can be seen below, showing if you know the name of the ship your ancestor was serving on, you may be able to find out additional information about their journey, including minor collisions, leaks and lost sails.

WRECKS AND CASUALTIES.

[COMPILED FROM OUR CORRESPONDENTS' REPORTS.]

AGANTYR, Larsen, which sailed from Cardiff Feb. 20 for Pensacola, has put back leaky.

ALPHA brig, Harding, has arrived at Sunderland from London, damaged, having been in collision with a galliot at the entrance of the Thames.

ANTONIO, Ollivier, arrived at Havre 1st inst. from Antofagasta, encountered most severe weather on the 15th and 16th Jan., in lat. 36 S, long. 28 W, which caused the vessel to labour heavily and make water; she also lost sails.

AFRICAINE, Giraud, which arrived at Liverpool Feb. 17 from Charleston, had encountered most severe weather, during which part of cargo (resin) was thrown overboard; the decks were swept, and the vessel sustained sundry damage.

AMITY brig, Scallan, of and from Limerick for Troon (ballast), which put into Longhope 16th ult., parted from both anchors on the 27th, and was run on the sand on the north side of that place. She sustained no damage, and would be got off next tide.

ADDER, of London, Bawyard, arrived at Aberdeen from Ipswich 2d inst., has lost bulwarks, &c.

An extract from the Shipping News column of the *Shipping and Mercantile Gazette* on 5 March 1874 detailing the incidents faced by named ships. (*Content provided by the British Library Board. All rights reserved. With thanks to The British Newspaper Archive (www.britishnewspaperarchive.co.uk)*)

Railway News

The birth of the railways was well covered by newspapers. Articles can be used to discover more about what rail travel was like during your ancestor's time. There is a huge number of reports regarding railway accidents, but also many about new railway lines being built, faster trains being implemented and miscellaneous reports about events that occurred while on the train or at a railway station.

The first railway line used by the public was the Stockton and Darlington railway opened in September 1825. This was a much-publicised event written about in national and local newspapers, including this report in the *Perthshire Courier* on 13 October 1825:

> The engine arrived at Stockton in three hours and seven minutes after leaving Darlington, including stops, the distance being nearly 12 miles, which is at the rate of four miles an hour ... the number of passengers in the waggons were counted about 550, and several more clung to the carriages on each side.

Using newspapers alone, it is hard to discover whether or not your ancestor travelled by train. Passengers and railway staff are usually only named if they are injured or killed in a train accident. There are rare cases where other names appear, however. In the early days of public rail travel, newspaper journalists interviewed passengers to get first-hand accounts of what the journey was like. People may also be named as the accused, victim or witness if a crime occurred on-board the train or at the station.

My fifth great-grandfather Robert Bugden was the stationmaster at Cheddington, Buckinghamshire in the mid-nineteenth century. He features in a range of articles, including being a witness to an accidental death on the tracks, being a witness to a man avoiding his train fare, being presented with a monetary award for twenty-five years' service as stationmaster and finding a large mushroom measuring 15 inches in circumference by the station! One of his last appearances in the newspapers was his death, which occurred at Farthinghoe railway station.

You may have found evidence from another source that your ancestor travelled by train. This is often seen in personal ephemera, such as diaries and postcards, recording their safe arrival at their destination. If you are aware of the date and locations of their travel, you can look up the timings and passenger information in local newspapers. The image below shows an example from the *Nottingham and Newark Mercury* on

THE Public are informed that on and after Monday the 5th of October next, a TRAIN for the conveyance of Third Class Passengers (in open carriages), Private Carriages, and Horses will leave the Euston Station, London, for Birmingham, every morning (except Sundays) at Seven o'Clock; and Birmingham, for London, every afternoon at Two o'Clock.

The Fares and Rates for the entire journey between London and Birmingham will be—

	£	s.	d.
Passengers	0	14	0
Private Carriages	3	0	0
Horse Boxes	4	0	0

And in proportion for intermediate distances.

The Train is appointed to leave the several Stations, as under:—

DOWN TRAIN.

Leaves

London	at 7 a. m.
Harrow	20 min. before 8
Watford	8
King's Langley	¼ past 8
Box Moor	½ past 8
Berkhampstead	¼ before 9
Tring	9
Cheddington	¼ past 9
Leighton	10
Bletchley and Fenny Stratford	25 min. after 10
Wolverton	¼ before 11
Roade	¼ past 12
Blisworth	¼ before 1
Weedon	¼ past 1
Crick and Welton	25 min. before 2
Rugby	2
Brandon	20 min. past 2
Coventry	20 min. before 3
Hampton	10 min. past 3
Arriving at Birmingham	about ¼ before 4 in the afternoon.

UP TRAIN.

Leaves

Birmingham	at 2 p. m.
Hampton	20 min. before 3
Coventry	20 min. past 3
Brandon	¼ before 4
Rugby	10 min. past 4
Crick and Welton	20 min. before 5
Weedon	5
Blisworth	20 min. past 5
Roade	¼ before 6
Wolverton	¼ past 6
Bletchley and Fenny Stratford	20 min. before 7
Leighton	25 min. after 7
Cheddington	¼ before 8
Tring	5 min. past 8
Berkhamstead	20 min. past 8
Box Moor	25 min. before 9
King's Langley	10 before 9
Watford	5 min. after 9
Harrow	¼ past 9
Arriving in London	about 10 in the evening.

Note.—Carriages and Horses will be required to be at the Stations at the least a quarter of an hour before the time of departure of the Train.

When the Stalls of the Horse Boxes are not filled, a Groom will be allowed to accompany the Horses in the Box free of charge.

Ample time will be allowed to Passengers for refreshment at the Roade Station, distant 60 miles from London.

An advertisement in *The Nottingham and Newark Mercury* dated 25 September 1840 for the London and Birmingham Railway with passenger information including timings and fares. *(Content provided by the British Library Board. All rights reserved. With thanks to The British Newspaper Archive (www. britishnewspaperarchive.co.uk))*

25 September 1840, giving times for each station and information for those travelling with their horses. This was very important in a time before motor vehicles and was a common scenario.

Other Forms of Travel

Besides ships and trains, your ancestor would have travelled on horse-drawn carts and possible other methods depending on the era, including trams, bicycles and, later on, motor vehicles. All will appear in articles with regard to accidents and technological improvements but a vast majority of day-to-day transport use goes unreported. The overlapping of these methods of travel during times of technological development can make for interesting reading to give context to your ancestor's life. A particular favourite angle of mine is to read articles from a time when horses and cars were first on the road together. Some of our ancestors would have seen the changing dynamics from the roads belonging to horses to the gradual passing over to the motor vehicle.

COMPETITION.—Now that cheap trains have restarted, char-a-banc proprietors have been obliged to reduce their charges to retain their popularity.—(*Sunday Illustrated.*)

An image of a charabanc with passengers, in the *Sunday Illustrated* on 17 July 1921 with a caption noting the need to reduce fares due to cheaper rail travel. (*Content provided by the British Library Board. All rights reserved. With thanks to The British Newspaper Archive (www.britishnewspaperarchive.co.uk)*)

In *Field* newspaper on 21 September 1901, an article describes one issue that may have faced our forebears:

> Although the automobile has for the last five years been legally recognised as having, with certain restrictions, a right to use the highways of this country, it is astonishing how few people have taken the trouble to accustom their horses to its presence … In more remote districts where the motor car is not to be met with every day, owners of horses still find equine equanimity considerably disturbed on the approach of an occasional automobile and with a curious lack of reason or justice, frequently blame the driver of the car for what is really their own fault.

Depending on the era in which you are researching, you may find other changes to travel that affected your ancestor. Charabancs used to be popular for sightseers and day trippers and changed from being horse-drawn to being motorised, before being phased out. You may find a photograph of your ancestor as a passenger in a charabanc in your own personal collection and wish to find out more. There are numerous articles and letters about the notorious rowdiness of many charabanc passengers, which also appears to have contributed to their downfall.

Whatever evidence you have of your ancestor using a particular mode of travel, research this in the newspaper for that period. There are articles about reliability, the cost of using such a form of travel and openings of new tram lines, for example. This can help us again to understand what the world was like for our ancestors in their everyday surroundings and what options were there for them if they needed to travel, whether that was short or long distance.

Chapter 10

ILLUSTRATIONS AND PHOTOGRAPHS

We all hope to find a drawing, painting or photograph of our ancestor. Seeing what their town or village looked like, what clothes they may have worn and the view of a crime scene they were involved in may also be on our genealogical wish list. Illustrations in newspapers were initially of very little use to family historians. These were generic black and white images, almost like a 'clip art' of the past, that were reused over and over and were fairly meaningless. Little illustration was used due to the complex and time-consuming printing techniques needed. Over time, these techniques gradually became cheaper and quicker allowing newspapers today to readily print clear colour photographs at a small price.

Some newspapers were developed specifically using illustrations as their selling point. These include *The Illustrated London News* which was issued weekly from 1847 to 1971 and then sporadically until 2003, and *The Graphic* published between 1869 and 1932. For most newspapers it was the beginning of the twentieth century when the number of images used began to increase fairly rapidly. Editors knew that pictures were attractive to readers and that images could quickly convey a news story to a potential buyer and entice them to make a purchase. Daily newspapers struggled to keep up with publishing images of recent events as they happened, whereas weekly publications had the advantage of having seven days to commission an artist to draw events of the week gone by.

For genealogists, the benefits of finding images in newspapers relevant to our family history is huge. They may be the only surviving source available which can show us an image of our ancestor. My husband's great-uncle Stewart Davidson died in a tobogganing accident at the age of 13 in 1931. The only photograph known to survive of him is one published in their local newspaper, *The Nottingham Evening Post*, in an article about the inquest. It is worth noting that to find the article I had to search under the different spelling of 'Stuart'; a reminder to try all spelling variations.

There are many reasons why a photograph of our ancestor may appear in a newspaper. Soldiers were commonly included in photograph sections of local newspapers where proud parents and wives sent them in alongside a brief biography. Photographs may also be included with an article about a notable birth, marriage or death. If your ancestor was involved in a crime, particularly as the accused, they may feature in an illustration or photograph. The more recent the newspaper the more likely they are to feature in an image. People in our tree from more recent generations may crop up in local articles about village fêtes, hobby clubs and fundraisers. My mum appears in a photograph, aged 10, in her local newspaper the *Woodbridge Reporter and Wickham Market Gazette* purchasing a jigsaw puzzle from the Excelsior Autumn band sale in 1964. If your ancestor was a photographer they may have had their work published in a newspaper – although credit is not always given.

As well as seeing photographs of our ancestors, images in newspapers can help us learn more about the time they were living in. We can see how different inventions and products were advertised to them, what the latest fashion looked like and gain a good idea of what different places looked like that were important to our ancestors. This could be their street, church, town hall, school, prison or farm. In the days before photography, illustrators would use their artistic licence to draw a newsworthy event, such as an assassination attempt on a well-known person or the sinking of a ship, using the facts that they had. When photography came into use, photographers had to learn how to frame a scene that was best for readers. Many newspapers, both national and local, often use images from their archives in a nostalgia feature. This can be a good chance to see an image that has been reprinted from the past but to a higher quality than it may have been originally. They may also use a different caption, meaning we have two chances to use the correct search term to find it.

Finding illustrations and photographs of interest to us in newspapers can be difficult. We need to think what terms may be used in the caption to get a result. Some websites, such as the British Newspaper Archive, allow you to narrow down results to those with illustrations in the article; however, this is not an accurate feature. Many results do not feature illustrations and some that do are incorrectly filtered out. Often, finding an image is a surprise to us when searching using our ancestor's name, whereas at other times we may go searching to find a specific event they were involved in. Trying a variety of search terms is key to finding images.

You will discover that in many newspapers both illustrations and photographs were often grouped together haphazardly on the same page. This made the printing experience a lot easier from the manufacturers' point of view. This means that rather than having a photograph included with a relevant story as we see today, historically the majority of images were grouped together. There are sporting images alongside pictures of those charged with murder, with royalty and images from plays seemingly with no order. Captions are still provided in these cases, which can help with identifying a person. As time went on and printing images became more common and easier to do, images appear in the manner we are accustomed to today.

Illustrations

Examples of some of the first illustrations were images of messengers and coats of arms used alongside the newspaper title. This can be seen on the front of many publications, such as *The Newcastle Courant* from its first issue in 1711 when a ship and messenger were pictured. In this title, the first letter of the first paragraph was also illustrated, again with a woodcut that could be reused. No other illustrations are found in these early issues. This is not an isolated case and is a fairly common find. *The Sherborne Mercury* from 1744 also used an illustrated first letter and two images either side of its title. The title itself is also decorated. The beautifully illustrated title page of *The Ipswich Journal* can be seen on the following page.

These commonly used early drawings were created using woodcuts. These were illustrations that had been cut into printing blocks that could be reused several times. These can be seen in very early news sheets, as well as multipage newspapers. As these woodcuts were reused frequently they were generic images. Rather than being of a specific person, they were of commonly required illustrations such as coats of arms, decorated letters and scenes that regularly featured in the news, such as a ship or a hanged criminal.

The earliest examples of illustrations that depicted a news story, and had been specifically commissioned, focused on well-known figures such as royalty and war heroes. These early illustrations were still woodcuts, however. The first illustration in *The Times* was 10 January 1806 when Lord Nelson's coffin was elaborately drawn, as well as his funeral carriage. The majority of illustrations seen in the early nineteenth

The illustrated title of *The Ipswich Journal* seen here on 13 May 1721. *(Content provided by the British Library Board. All rights reserved. With thanks to The British Newspaper Archive (www.britishnewspaperarchive.co.uk))*

century, however, were logos used in advertisements. These can be of relevance, particularly where they are used to advertise a company associated with our ancestor. These images can be a great tangible feature to include in our ancestor's story.

There are several other early nineteenth-century examples of illustrations. One is an engraving of Sir Robert Wilson, Captain John Hely-Hutchinson and Michael Bruce who appeared on the third page of *The Sun* on 16 May 1816 after their trial for treason in France. This highlights that illustrations did not always feature on the front page, with there being no other illustrations in this issue aside from a sun in the title. Drawings of named people in the news and particular events did not start to become popular until the mid-nineteenth century. The popularity had begun to accelerate after Queen Victoria's coronation in 1838, after numerous newspapers included a portrayal of the event, but the main reason for the number of illustrations increasing around this time was down to improvements in newspaper printing technology. This made it quicker and cheaper for newspaper companies to print images. Prior to the mid-nineteenth century, illustrations tended to have thick lines (often blotchy in appearance) that took a long time to print onto paper. Thanks to the printing advancements in the 1840s, newspaper images from then on had a much clearer appearance. You are therefore much more likely to find an illustration relating to your ancestor from the 1840s onwards and, where found, this is normally clear.

There are many examples where the digitisation process has made images appear blurry or shadowed. This can happen with newspapers of any age. In these cases, try searching other sites for the same title. Different websites have scanned different copies of the same issue so a clearer image may be found elsewhere. Alternatively, you can try to source an original paper copy.

GIRL'S STRUGGLE WITH SCAR-FACED MAN NEAR ILKLEY CRIME SCENE

Illustrations from the front cover of *The Illustrated Police News* on 24 October 1929 showing the attack of Nancy Richardson at Ilkley. The attack happened eight days prior to the images being published. (*Content provided by the British Library Board. All rights reserved. With thanks to The British Newspaper Archive (www. britishnewspaperarchive.co.uk)*)

Illustrations, particularly up until the late nineteenth century, were often delayed appearing in newspapers. While editors of daily newspapers would have preferred a drawing of an event that happened the previous day to appear in their title, it simply was not possible to commission an artist to draw a scene, transfer this to an engraving and then get it printed overnight ready for publication. When searching for an illustration, therefore, be sure to expand your search dates for a few weeks after an event. The Great Sheffield Flood occurred on 11 March 1864 but it was not until 26 March that related drawings appeared in *The Illustrated London News*.

You are more likely to have luck finding an illustration of your ancestor if they were well known within their community or involved in a high-profile event, such as a natural disaster, a royal occasion or a railway accident. Artists often depicted real-life people, such as vicars, doctors and mayors where they attended a scene. The majority of people portrayed, however, will be nonspecific figures from the artist's imagination. Nevertheless, where an event, newsworthy enough to be illustrated, happened in your ancestor's locality, this can be a great insight into life in their time and the sights they would have seen. There will always be an element of artistic licence used; however, illustrations help bring history to life in a time before photography could be used in newspapers.

Cartoons

One important type of illustration in newspapers is the cartoon. The most common subjects of editorial cartoons, particularly historically speaking, are political figures. They can therefore be of most use to researchers looking into any political figures in their family tree, or anyone else of note, including royalty and other aristocrats. While this appears to discount most of us, myself included, they can still be of great interest. Although most illustrators in newspapers aimed to provide an accurate depiction of a person or an event, a cartoonist had the ability to exaggerate a person's features, dramatise an event and highlight the general public feeling towards a topic at the time. Subjects of cartoons tend to surround the most talked-about subjects of the week and the opinion given is usually one which most of their readers would agree with; if you do find a cartoon, bear in mind the political leaning of that particular newspaper title.

A cartoon usually aims to put a humorous spin on a topic in the news while either reflecting public opinion or trying to influence it. During the world wars, cartoons were also used as morale boosters. It can be appealing to view cartoons to see what our ancestors may have been feeling towards the issues of their day. We may have to read several articles about a news story to understand what a cartoon could convey to us in seconds. Arguably, cartoons will be of most interest to those researching their cartoonist ancestors. Few people have the opportunity to gain an insight into our ancestor's political and social views in the same way.

Also featuring in newspapers are comic strips. These tend to be less politically charged and have little use to us for genealogical purposes, but you may still wish to see what was amusing in their day. They may also hint at what domestic life was like at the time and attitudes towards certain sections of society.

Photographs

Finding a photograph of our ancestor is a true highlight in genealogical research. It is certainly special to see the face of a person whom we have researched for so long and know so much about. The appearance of an ancestor can also tell us a lot about them. This could include any scars, their weight, their clothing which may hint at their financial status and other physical features of interest, such as their hairstyle and facial hair. Newspapers are one of many sources where we may find a photograph of our ancestor.

It was the French publication *L'Illustration* that claimed the record for publishing the first photograph in a newspaper in 1848, although *The Illustrated London News* was not far behind. Both photographs were printed as engravings due to the technology of the time. In 1880, the Americans invented the halftone printing process where black and white photographs could be recreated using tiny dots of different shades of grey and black. *The Illustrated London News* was regularly printing photographs in their publication from the early 1890s. You would be lucky to find such a photograph relevant to your ancestor from this period. In the early days of photography in newspapers, most images were of well-known people who readers would be interested in seeing, such as royalty, politicians and actors.

The technological improvements needed to mass produce photographs in newspapers developed at the beginning of the twentieth century. *The Daily Mirror* was first published in 1903 and early on gained a reputation for its use of illustrations. This soon developed into the use of photography also. It famously managed to print two photographs of the funeral of Prince George, Duke of Cambridge on its cover on 23 March 1904, the day after the event. It is hard to imagine what a fascinating glimpse into historical events this must have been for our ancestors, when for us seeing photographs of a royal family member or celebrity is so normal today. Photographs had been used inside newspapers before this but not with such speed in reporting.

At this point, printing photographs in newspapers was still a costly process that took a long time to complete. This means in the very early twentieth-century, photographs were usually only printed by national newspapers rather than local publications. Unless your ancestor was a noteworthy figure you are unlikely to find a photograph of them printed in a newspaper until slightly later, when the technology became quicker and cheaper to use.

Photography in newspapers began to appear more commonly in every publication from the early to mid-twentieth century. It is therefore the more recent generations of our forebears who we are more likely to find photographs of. The benefit of photography over illustration is that there was less room for artistic licence. A person in a crowd in an illustration was simply a generic figure, whereas a person in a crowd in a photograph was a real person. Historically, photographs were printed as they were taken, with little to no editing other than cropping. Today we need to be more careful to ensure the image we are looking at is real rather than AI-generated and, if it is a true photograph, consider that it may have been heavily edited.

Photographs were widely employed during the First World War (1914–1919) and the Second World War (1939–1945). Censorship obviously prevented a lot of the true conditions of the battlefront from reaching the public at home; however, we can still use newspaper photography to research our wartime ancestors. Photographs could include portraits of soldiers sent to local newspapers, scenes of devastation after an air raid, and troops during time off. The latter can be interesting to view, such as football games with players still in their uniforms.

That being said, photographs of our ancestors can be notoriously difficult to discover in newspapers. If your ancestor appears with a caption including their name this will appear in a normal search. Soldiers were usually named according to their rank. Try searching for 'Cpl. J. Shears' rather than John Shears for example. If your ancestor appears in a group, their name may or may not be given. Local newspapers like to name individuals as it is more likely to increase sales. National newspapers are less likely to name people in a group unless they are noteworthy. With this in mind, think about which groups your ancestor was in and use them as a search term. This could be anything from their military regiment, to their WI group, to their sporting team. There are hundreds of thousands of photographs in newspapers featuring unnamed people.

A photograph in *The Berwick Journal* on 8 July 1915 of British Prisoners of War held at Doeberitz, Germany. George Coulter sent this photograph home to his mother and is named as standing on the far right of the image. Only three other soldiers are named in the caption. Searching for the name of the PoW camp would bring up a positive result. *(Content provided by the British Library Board. All rights reserved. With thanks to The British Newspaper Archive (www. britishnewspaperarchive.co.uk))*

Of course, to be able to recognise them, we need to know what they looked like to start with.

As well as photographs of people, we can use photographs of scenes to great use too, in the same way as we can for illustrations. Photographs are generally more trustworthy and give a view of the scene as it was; however, the photographer could still choose exactly what part of a scene he wished to take. Editors could also choose to crop a section of a photograph off, if they did not want it to be printed.

For a photograph to appear in a national newspaper, it usually required the news story to be of major public interest. This includes natural disasters or mass occupational accidents, such as mining disasters and war scenes. If your ancestor was involved in such an incident, try searching using the name of the place it occurred along with the date that it happened. Famous people would be photographed in newspapers regularly, including politicians, royalty, actors and singers. These are usually captioned with their name.

Local newspapers also included photographs of national news stories but over time began to print images of local scenes. This could include local weddings, village fêtes, church interiors and exteriors and prize-givings. Again, the nature of the image will determine whether a person is named or not. Wedding photographs will name the bride and groom; in contrast, village fete scenes will not usually name individuals within the photograph. More recently, relatives have sent in photographs to local newspapers to celebrate milestone birthdays and anniversaries; these will be named and can be a great way of finding images of distant cousins.

Colour photography is a more recent invention. Scotland's *Daily Record* was one of the first newspapers to print a colour photograph, in 1936, while *The Banbury Guardian* was the first newspaper in Britain to use a colour photograph on its front page in 1962. *The Illustrated London News* printed beautiful colour photographs on its double-page centre spread in the 1930s. Colour photography became more commonly used in newspapers gradually from the 1960s and then, again with an improvement in technology and a cheaper cost, more common again from the 1990s. This means only our most recent relatives may be found in colour in newspapers. While there are many apps, computer programs and personalised services offering to colourise black and white images these tend not to work well with black and white newspaper images.

The quality of many photographs in historical newspapers is quite poor. Faces can be hard to recognise and zooming in on the image leaves it looking highly pixelated. Many have a darker-than-normal appearance, often due to the scanning settings that were used to digitise the newspaper to make the text clearer to read. In this situation, you can try searching for a copy of the same issue on another newspaper digitisation website or locate a physical copy. It is also worth searching other websites, depending on the subject. Many military photographs featured in newspapers can be found on the Imperial War Museums Collection page at **www.iwm. org.uk/collections**. You can opt to search for digitised media and filter further by photographs. I have found many military photographs printed in newspapers in their collection and they are extremely clear.

It is worth remembering that historical photographs can be printed at any time, rather than the time they were taken. Newspapers often do

Ampthill couple

Miss Diane Elizabeth Woodward, younger daughter of Mrs. V. Woodward, Linsleigh, Station Road, Ampthill, and of the late Mr. F. E. Woodward, was married on Saturday at Ampthill Parish Church to Mr. Ronald Ingle, younger son of Mrs. K. Ingle, of 5 Bedford Street, Ampthill, and of the late Mr. J. O. Ingle.

The ceremony was performed by the Rev. R. G. H. Cooper, and it was followed by a reception at the White Hart, Ampthill.

The couple left for a honeymoon touring in the West Country. Mr. and Mrs. Ingle will make their future home at 59 Bedford Street, Ampthill.

A beautiful photograph of a couple on their wedding day as seen in *Ampthill News* on 28 March 1961. *(Content provided by the British Library Board. All rights reserved. With thanks to The British Newspaper Archive (www. britishnewspaperarchive.co.uk))* comparison slides of what people or places used to look like and what they look like now. Readers can also choose to submit their own historical images of interest to be printed where relevant. This is particularly common in provincial newspapers. The image below is a wedding photograph of my great-grandmother's sister Florence Hatcher and her husband, William Brewer. The photo was taken in 1912 but was printed in the local newspaper in 1991 after their son Bill sent the editor of Dorset's *Daily Echo* a copy to feature it in their Bygone Days page. It is worth noting that the caption incorrectly names the bride's mother as Mary, rather than Elizabeth; a reminder to not take everything in print as it is given.

A final issue to consider with regard to photographs is identification within a group of people. Historical captions, and even some today, are not especially clear with naming people in an obvious manner. If there are two rows of people they may be named with the front row first left to right, followed by the back row left to right. Where the manner in which they have been named is clear, this is very helpful; what is less useful is where people are standing in a disorderly group and names are given. It can be hard, sometimes impossible, to know which person in the photograph each name refers to. If you have no idea what the person looks like, it is worth saving the photograph in the hope you might come across another one day so you know which one they are. You may be able to rule some people in a group out, such as those of the wrong sex or people who are identified by their clothing, such as a mayor or soldier.

A family photo from the Hatcher/Brewer wedding taken in 1911. This was printed eighty years later in the *Daily Echo* on 2 January 1991. (*Image author's own*)

Chapter 11

MISCELLANEOUS ARTICLES AND FEATURES

Nonconformity

Most of us will discover we have some Nonconformist ancestors. For the most part, researching them in newspapers is the same as researching those who followed the Church of England. Many newspapers have their roots in Nonconformity, such as *The Guardian* which was established in 1821 as *The Manchester Guardian* by a group of dissenters. *The Leeds Mercury* also has a Nonconformist background. There can be a religious influence to this, with topics on racing and gambling not being reported as the writers and editors, and much of their readership, did not agree with these topics.

As well as these larger newspapers, there are thousands of other Nonconformist newspapers, journals, magazines and periodicals. Not all have survived and not all are yet available to search online. There were many notable publications, such as *The Nonconformist* from 1841–1880, *The Methodist Times* 1885–1902 and *The Jewish Record* 1868–1871. Many of these titles published their own birth, marriage and death columns as well as obituaries for those who followed their faith. Ministers in particular were frequently written about, as well as those who lived to an old age having followed the particular denomination for much of their life. Their dedication to their chapel is often noted.

The example on the following page, from *The Methodist Times*, is a classic example of how a death of a Nonconformist is reported. These short obituaries can provide much background into a person's life, in particular their beliefs and details about the religion that they followed. Here, the death of Lewis Davis of Ferndale is noted with details of his education, work, character and funeral. The article observes that he was 'an earnest Wesleyan Methodist'. The chapel he attended is also named; this is more

DEATH OF MR. LEWIS DAVIS, OF FERNDALE.

We greatly regret to record the death of Mr. Lewis Davis, of Ferndale, which took place at Langland 'Castle, near the Mumbles, last Sunday, at five a.m. Mr. Davis passed peacefully away in the presence of his family. The cause of death was disease of the spinal cord. He was educated at Wesley College, Sheffield, under the care of the late Dr. Waddy. Mr. Davis's collieries at Ferndale are among the most extensive and gigantic in existence. Last year his total exports reached considerably over a million tons of coal. Mr. Davis enjoyed in a remarkable degree the confidence and affection of his workmen. When the great strike took place in 1871 he was among the earliest and most assiduous workers in promoting an amicable settlement. Mr. Davis had in his employ 3,500 workmen, so that nearly 18,000 persons were dependent on his enterprise for their daily sustenance. Mr. Davis was often greatly pressed to accept a seat in Parliament for one of the South Wales constituencies, but his retiring disposition led him to shrink from public life, although he was an excellent and polished speaker. Mr. Davis was an earnest Wesleyan Methodist, and regularly attended the Welsh Chapel at Ferndale. He was a great friend of the Rev. Mark Guy Pearse, who dedicated his last published work to him. He took a deep interest in the West Central Mission, and his lamented death has deprived that enterprise of one who would probably have given it munificent support. His funeral will take place this afternoon.

A short biography of Lewis Davis written upon his death in *The Methodist Times* on 5 Jan 1888. It is noted that Lewis was a Wesleyan Methodist who attended the Welsh Chapel at Ferndale. *(Content provided by the British Library Board. All rights reserved. With thanks to The British Newspaper Archive (www. britishnewspaperarchive.co.uk))*

common than naming which church a Church of England follower attended in a similar article.

As well as using the traditional online search methods, you can use your ancestor's surname and their denomination as search terms together, such as 'Methodist Barker', narrowing the results down by county if necessary. If you know the chapel they attended, you can also use this as a search term to see what news occurred there, such as meetings, memorial services, or incidents such as fire. You may also find reports from when the building was erected or when it closed down, perhaps with comments from ministers and followers.

Searching for your ancestor's chosen denomination in regular newspapers from their day may tell you the attitude towards them at the time. Local newspapers, in particular, can hint towards any warm or ill feelings towards a particular group of people. Some denominations collaborated to achieve particular goals. You may find additional chapels being built in the area due to increased demand and popularity. If you discover particular ill feelings towards your ancestor's religion, this may hint at why they moved away from a certain area at a particular time.

As an example of how newspapers helped me to break down a brick wall in my own family tree, I was aware that my Blundell line were Nonconformists in the late eighteenth and early nineteenth century. Samuel Townley Blundell and Rebecca Turner were married on 9 June 1782 in their local Church of England parish church, as was necessary for their marriage to be legally recognised at that time, but their burials and baptisms of their children could not be found. This is a classic sign of Nonconformity. However, I was unsure exactly what religion they followed. As so few records are transcribed or available online, any search result online drew a blank. In the end, the problem was solved by researching the name of the executor of Samuel's will, named Stephen Warwick. Again, initially a search on genealogy databases did not give much away – he appeared to be an unassuming farmer. A search on the newspaper database, however, gave an instant result. Stephen was the Baptist Minister of Roade Chapel for thirty-four years – problem solved! From this I then went on to find Samuel's name in the members list of Roade Baptist Chapel and it gave me a new avenue upon which to research the family.

House History

Researching a house history is closely linked to researching your family history. Many of the same sources, such as census returns, maps and title deeds, are used. Newspapers can also be included in this list. Some people wish to research the history of their own house to see what newsworthy events occurred there. Others wish to research the house history of one of their ancestors to see who lived there before and after their residence. This can be a useful genealogical task as you may discover relatives living there before or after them. Researching a house history can also lead you to discover documents about your ancestor that you may not otherwise have found, as they may not be named in a catalogue but their residence may be.

The most obvious way to research a house history via historical newspapers is to use the address as a search term. The same issues apply here as when searching using a name with regard to OCR transcription, so you may wish to try numerous spelling variations. Be aware that house numbers of many roads have changed over the years so ensure you are tracing the right number for the right date.

You may wish to research a house history prior to the introduction of house numbers. This makes the task much trickier, particularly when using newspapers as a source. You will discover that street names are useful and frequently named even when house numbers are not.

Again, street names have changed over time so be sure to check you are researching the right road in the right town or village. Some news will be relevant to a house where only the street is named, such as rivers flooding and the introduction of street lighting. Infrastructure news about improvements to sewage works and road works in the street are notable to house history. The property you are searching for may, at times, have a house name rather than a number. This house name can change. This search term is particularly effective when you are researching the history of a public house, with the name of the pub a useful search tool. This is also the same for similar establishments, such as hotels.

If you are researching a property on a new development these are commonly reported in local newspapers. Larger projects, such as new towns like Milton Keynes, were reported on nationally. It can be interesting to read the attitudes of locals and the general public with regard to these new developments. Alternatively, you may be researching a house history only to discover that the property no longer stands. There are often articles about house demolition and slum clearances which will provide details of dates.

As well as researching the history of a particular house, many choose to research the history of other properties built on the same plot. Newspapers can be useful for detailing when earlier properties were lost. The example below from Liverpool's *The Albion* on 23 November 1846 names two streets and explains that a recently built house was rather oddly 'blown down'.

When you have gathered together a thorough house history for a property and know the names and dates of who lived there and when, you can then use these as search terms. If you know Joseph Stickland lived in the property from 1871–1881 you can search for his name and parish and narrow the dates down to see what he got up to during this period. While the residence itself may not be named or described, articles may still imply new information with regard to house history.

As seen in the Advertisements chapter, you of course can also use historical newspapers to track down any businesses that were run from

> At Birkenhead a newly-built house, at the corner of Chester-street and Ivy-street, the property of Mr. Walters, was blown down, but, providentially, no person was near at the time.

In a report on a recent severe storm, the loss of a property is noted with two streets named and the owner of the property in Liverpool's *The Albion* on 23 November 1846. (*Public Domain*) the address, property listings, a householder advertising for a new servant and details of related auctions. Property listings often state how old the house is and describe its layout at the time of sale, including any gardens and outbuildings.

Politics

Politics has always featured heavily in newspapers. Whether readers wanted to find out more about national or local politics, it was important that editors published the latest updates. In a general sense, it is useful to discover more about changes to national legislation to see how it may have affected our ancestors and the public opinion of the time. It can also be of interest to read about the economic climate at the time to see if this can help us understand why our ancestors were struggling, why they relocated or why they may have ended up in the workhouse. While almost all newspapers feature politics to some degree, some are more focused on certain parties or beliefs than others. Examples include *The Suffragette* 1912–1918 and *The Rhondda Socialist Newspaper* of 1911–1914.

Looking more specifically for named ancestors, you will be in luck if your ancestor stood for a political position – whether that was on the local council or a government standing. Prior to an election, you will be able to find out much about your ancestor's beliefs, what they were standing for and usually a brief biography including details of their education and work background. This helped the readership decide who to vote for. Published election results in newspapers will tell you how successful your ancestor was and demonstrate what percentage of the voting public sided with them over other candidates.

Your ancestor may be named as being politically active in their local area. This could include evidence of them being present at political rallies, protests or attending a local governmental meeting. You may also be lucky and come across a list of members of a named political organisation. At other times, public petitions appeared in newspapers naming those who have signed it thus far. Finding your ancestor's name in any of these cases can tell you what they believed in and how strongly they believed it.

You may be aware that your ancestor was involved in a political movement such as Chartism or women's suffrage. You can search local newspapers for events they may have partaken in for such causes. Alternatively, you may be unaware they believed in such a cause but find them named in an article, perhaps in court accused of malicious acts to highlight their plight. The article below is from the *Dundee Evening Telegraph* dated 16 September 1908 and names four suffragettes

RELEASE OF SUFFRAGETTES TO-DAY.

Enthusiastically Greeted at Prison Gates.

Four members of the Women's Social and Political Union who went to prison for three months in connection with the raid on the House of Commons on June 30 were this morning released from Holloway Gaol.

They were Miss Haig, Miss Joachim (niece of the well-known pianist), Miss Elsie Howey, and Miss Vera Wentworth. They were enthusiastically greeted at the prison gates by a large number of their comrades, and proceeded in procession to the Queen's Hall, where they had breakfast.

The names of four suffragettes are given upon their release from Holloway Gaol in *Dundee Evening Telegraph* on 16 September 1908. *(Content provided by the British Library Board. All rights reserved. With thanks to The British Newspaper Archive (www.britishnewspaperarchive.co.uk))*

by surname who have been released from Holloway Gaol. Genealogical information is given for one lady, telling us she is the niece of a well-known pianist.

By the mid-nineteenth century, newspapers began to understand more about the views of their audience and became involved in campaigns for change in legislation and raising awareness for certain issues. We still see this today with journalists publishing one-sided stories about a hot topic of the day, sometimes having carried out their own research and interviews. These stories sell well to the public, hence their continuation. Where they feature on the front page, editors need to be careful to ensure they are not alienating too many of their readers with a controversial opinion. Stories such as these can give us information as to what may have driven changes to certain laws, particularly ones that affected our ancestors. Examples of such reports include the investigation, by *The Sunday Times*, into the side effects of using thalidomide in the 1960s, and reports influencing the repeal of the Corn Laws in the 1840s, such as those in *The Manchester Guardian*. A series of controversial articles titled by their author William Thomas Stead as '*The Maiden Tribute of Modern Babylon*' highlighted child prostitution in London in the *Pall Mall Gazette* in 1885 and resulted in the age of consent being raised from 13 to 16. These are hugely shocking reports to read and can educate readers on the issue of child trafficking in the capital in the nineteenth century.

The Workhouse

It is common to discover that your ancestor spent some time in the workhouse, either through viewing a workhouse register or it being their place of death on a death certificate. Their stay may only have been short or they may have spent a great deal of their life going in and out of the workhouse until they died while resident there. Searching the name of the workhouse in local newspapers from the time that they stayed there can give you details such as their diet, punishments, sanitary conditions and any recent scandals. There were reviews of workhouse rations as well as reports on the weekly or fortnightly meetings of the Board of Guardians. The reports are believed to be purposefully negative in an attempt to deter people from entering the workhouse, which was seen as a last resort by authorities.

The Andover workhouse scandal of the 1840s is a good example of how newspapers can pick up on a story and gain great publicity for a particular social cause. At one of the weekly board meetings regarding Andover workhouse, one of the Poor Law Guardians, Hugh Munday, reported that he had heard rumours that service users were so hungry that they were being driven to gnaw marrow and gristle from rotting bones that were given to them to make fertiliser. Munday then began to escalate the issue higher until it reached parliament. This news then reached the press and awareness grew, as well as new allegations.

These new allegations were very serious, involving the sexual assault and rape of female inmates by the master, as well as accusations of his drunkenness and theft of provisions, including their rations. Ultimately, the inquiry was suspended leaving researchers with an uncertain outcome. If your ancestor was resident at Andover during the mid-1840s, it is worth researching the scandal to see if they were interviewed and to hear how other inmates described their time there. Other similar stories can be found in local newspaper reports.

A typical newspaper report on a Board of Guardians meeting at Pewsey can be seen in *The Devizes and Wiltshire Advertiser* on

28 September 1899. The names of all those attending the meeting are given first followed by accepted tenders, such as receiving milk at a cost of 10d a gallon from Mr Holmes. A list of the issues discussed then follows. This includes a report that 9-year-old inmate Jack Yates had stolen 4½d from a fellow inmate. His punishment was decided to be 'two strokes with the birch, in front of the other lads in the house', no doubt as a deterrent to others.

Infectious diseases were discussed at these meetings, although in this case it is simply noted none were present. If you are aware your ancestor died in the workhouse of an infectious disease, such as smallpox, tuberculosis or cholera, research the most recent Board of Guardians meeting to see if the news features. Your forebear may have been the only person to die of that known cause that week or there may have been many, giving us a clearer picture of what their last days were like.

Other workhouse issues that may be of interest are reports on hygiene, descriptions of types of labour partaken by healthy inmates, descriptions of the building's layout and changes in the law and reform. While we can read from other sources about when workhouse laws were changed, reading newspaper articles gives us a great insight into why they were changed, including interviews with current and previous inmates and Guardians. There are multiple accounts of individuals' stories, although in some cases these people are not named. For example, in the *Totnes Weekly Times* on 16 October 1886 an article states: 'One of the delegates mentioned an instance in which six children deserted by their parents had to be sent to six separate unions because each of the poor little victims had been born in a different parish. It was a cruel thing to separate these poor deserted children under such circumstances.' You may suspect this relates to your family and be unable to prove it, but at least it explains to the researcher why the children were separated.

In the interest of balance and to show that not all workhouse reports were negative, there is a lovely update in *The West London Observer* on 31 December 1897 regarding Christmas Day in the Kensington workhouse. This describes how the wards were festively decorated and residents were provided with a Christmas dinner of beef with plum pudding. Entertainment was provided in the evening. Perhaps some of our workhouse inmates were lucky enough to enjoy such a meal while a resident there. The article on the following page shows how some reports about the workhouse can provide useful information, including the ages of named inmates, the length of their stay and their previous occupation.

SOME WORKHOUSE INMATES.

Inquiries made into the Christmas festivities at the workhouses brought to light some interesting facts regarding inmates of many of these institutions who have "seen better days." In the Fulham Union Workhouse, for instance, is a comparatively young man, who was formerly a stockbroker in the City, renting offices at £300 a year. He fell in love with a young lady of good position, but his father—still living in Surrey—objected to the marriage. The result was that the young man, in his disappointment, speculated heavily, and lost all his money. Another inmate was formerly a governess in several titled families.

Marylebone Workhouse, where Mr. Gladstone's old butler is still the porter, and in receipt of a regular weekly sum from the ex-Prime Minister, contains no less than two hundred and seventy-six out of 1,800 inmates who are over eighty years of age, the oldest being a lady of ninety-eight, Mrs. Sarah Warwick, who has been in the institution for forty years. Her companion, Annie Guest, is ninety-four, and sitting with them at the table on Christmas Day were three other old ladies, the united ages of all five amounting to four hundred and forty-three years.

Some 1,200 inmates of the Kensington Workhouse included a Dr. H. Weymouth, an eminent physiologist of the University of Giessen, now seventy years old, who in his more prosperous days acted as tutor to the children of many distinguished persons in England and abroad. Another inmate is the widow of a Hussar captain who at one time acted as tutor to a Duchess. In the City of London Workhouse at Homerton is an ex-commercial traveller, who lost several thousand pounds in the Liberator collapse, and who is now anxious to get employment. The Hackney Union Workhouse has among its 2,573 inmates an artist who used to be "hung" at the Royal Academy. Holborn boasts an old lady inmate of one hundred and two years, who talks freely of the Great Frost and the Waterloo victory.

An article from *Henley & South Oxfordshire Standard* on 31 December 1897 giving details of multiple workhouse inmates' lives, albeit not all by name, which makes it much harder to find. (*Content provided by the British Library Board. All rights reserved. With thanks to The British Newspaper Archive (www.britishnewspaperarchive.co.uk)*)

Extracts from Pedigrees and Other Sources

National and local newspapers include extracts from other publications. This can be anything from political leaflets, books, religious sermons and poetry. Most useful to us as family historians are where genealogical sources are transcribed. This is not an overly common find; however, you can find multiple examples where parish registers, wills and pedigrees are transcribed. As with any transcription, these should be treated with caution and the original source should always be sought to confirm the details printed in the newspaper.

The Buckingham Express published multiple extracts from Buckingham's parish registers in a series in 1911–1912, including in the issue dated 30 December 1911 when the parish's baptisms for 1631–1633 are transcribed. For 1633, baptisms include John Paxon, son of Nicholas, baptised on 3 March and Elizabeth Robins, daughter of John, baptised on 7 April. There are numerous other similar examples, often published purely for local interest.

Genealogy became a popular topic and a subject of curiosity, particularly from the late nineteenth century. This is reflected in provincial newspapers, some of which even had a 'genealogy corner' or 'Ancestry' column where readers could request information about their forebears. In *The Cornish and Devon Post* on 24 September 1881, a complex pedigree of the Corrie family of Bude can be found dating back to the sixteenth century. This also incorporates extracts from parish registers. Unfortunately, we cannot take any of these pedigrees as fact without sourcing the original material, in the same way that we cannot copy another person's online family tree without checking every single individual source. Thoroughness is key in genealogy and where multiple facts are presented to us in one source, we must be careful to do our own research.

Letters to the Editor

You may hit the newspaper research jackpot and discover a letter written by your ancestor that was published in a local or national newspaper. The subject matter could be absolutely anything they wished but highlights the fact that this was clearly an issue that was important to them. There are many that were submitted anonymously or using a pseudonym, making the author, unfortunately, untraceable. Others only give initials, whereas some give their full name and parish of residence. There are also some in local newspapers where a street address is given but no name.

Letters that were submitted to newspapers were often edited before publishing. This remains the case today. You are therefore not necessarily reading the exact wording your ancestor submitted, but the majority will be and the gist of the letter will be the same. Grammar and spelling are the most likely things that will have been altered, and the wording may be reduced to fit within a certain space. Therefore, if you do find a letter from an ancestor, bear in mind that you cannot use this as evidence of their writing level as their spelling and grammar may have been significantly altered. Not all letters that were sent to the editor were published, meaning many have been lost.

The subjects in letters vary wildly in newspapers. The majority in national newspapers surround the bigger news stories of the moment, such as changes in legislation and crime levels. Some of the breaking news stories of the past were actually broken via a correspondent's letter with the editor seemingly requiring no further proof before printing the story. Letters in local newspapers touch on national stories, but also focus on local topics of interest. These are not always discussing news stories, but are often simply comments that they wished to share with an audience. There are noise complaints, reports of minor local crimes, requests for charity donations and letters from businesses advertising their services. The subject could be almost anything as long as the editor deemed it suitable for publication. You may find a debate occurring where the same two or more people reply to each other continuously via the letters page regarding a topic of controversy.

Amusingly, you will find the topics are often much the same as today, including the criticism of somebody's grammar. In the *Nottingham and Midland Counties Daily Express* on 29 January 1877, an anonymous letter writer sent in:

A writer in the columns of a London paper says 'I have had various inquiries made me.' Now how can any inquiries make him? This is a sort of phrase, 'vile phrase', as Shakespeare says, which is quite as bad as 'I wrote him'. How could he 'wrote him' … I hope the Board schools will look after these solecisms.

Some letters give family details, such as names of their parents, spouse and children; however, for the majority of letters, the usefulness for us as researchers lies in the subject matter. A person would not write a letter to a newspaper unless the issue at hand was important to them. You could discover any number of details about a forebear, such as their political persuasion, their detest for a building of a new railway line, or their gratitude towards somebody local who helped them in a time of distress. Letters are a lovely personal touch to discover within a newspaper and can often be found, unexpectedly, simply when searching for an ancestor's name.

In general terms, browsing the letters of the local newspaper can make for interesting reading to see what the hot topics were at the time. Always remember that a letter from one person is not representative of what the majority of the public thought or felt. One anonymous letter published in the *Birmingham Mail* on 6 October 1906 states: 'I too am thrown out of employment because a woman agreed to do the work a bit cheaper. If things go on like this much longer every man will be staying at home doing housework while his wife goes out to earn the weekly wage.' Letters are generally less filtered than articles written by paid journalists and can be an interesting insight. Unfortunately, these insights are sometimes reflective of the intolerant attitudes of the past.

Village Fêtes

Whether you are searching for a named ancestor or the name of a particular parish, you may come across reports in provincial newspapers regarding village fêtes. The detail of these can vary from being a few lines long to being very detailed with names of prize winners, judges, notable attendees, stallholders and entertainers. It is widely believed many of our forebears met their spouses at fêtes when people from surrounding villages would attend, although this is hard to prove for specific people.

Fête reports can give a great picture of the day, including timings of the events of the day, weather conditions, performances from local choirs and dance groups, and details of charitable fundraising. Fêtes were extremely popular local events that at least some of your ancestors would have been sure to attend. While the majority of attendees will not be named in newspapers, many are, including children. My grandmother Gwendoline Keep is named as having correctly guessed the weight of a cake at Steeple Claydon fête in the *Buckingham Advertiser and North Bucks Free Press* on 24 September 1932 when she was 9 years old.

Competitions have long been a key part of a local fête. Prizes were handed out for the biggest vegetables, neatest needlework, straightest hat trimming and the best flower arrangement, among many other very varied categories. Sport also featured heavily with several races of differing classes. There are the typical races you would expect, such as egg and spoon races and children's races, but also races only for married women, races for bandsmen while they play their instruments, and chasing greased pigs. You may find similar reports regarding jubilee celebrations, town fairs and horticultural shows. In more modern times, local newspapers feature photographs of these events.

Lodges, Groups and Clubs

You may have an ancestor who was a member of a lodge, such as a Freemason's lodge, Oddfellows group or a similar club. Reports on their meetings feature frequently in newspapers, as well as appointments of officers and dinners. Some reports give full lists of attendees, although their name may be given as 'Brother Read' rather than William Read for example, depending on their title within the group. There are notices of upcoming meetings, as well as detailed reports given afterwards. These include speeches that were given, awards given, such as those to long-standing members, and mentions of recently deceased members. If you are aware of the lodge or group that your ancestor was a member of, and the years that they attended, you can use the name to search for newspaper articles in the local newspaper. These reports are often very lengthy, giving great detail of each meeting. It is common to see relationships stated between members, usually when a son was initiated into his father's lodge.

Puzzles and Competitions

From a curiosity stand point, you may wish to view the puzzles in newspapers from your ancestor's time. Crosswords appeared in British newspapers from the mid-1920s onwards and it can be interesting to see the level of education the editors believed their readers to have. Other puzzles and competitions appeared much earlier, in the nineteenth century. Even if you are aware that your ancestor was an avid reader of a named newspaper, however, it does not necessarily mean that they completed the crossword or even had any interest in it whatsoever. From a general point of view, they are still interesting to peruse.

You may also discover your ancestor won a puzzle competition. Sometimes there was a fee for entering which helped the newspaper to cover costs. The puzzle competition could be anything from a crossword, spot the ball or an illustrated chess game. If your ancestor did win, check the previous issue to see the puzzle that won them the prize and have a go yourself to see how you would fare against them! While it was certainly harder in our ancestor's day to cheat – compared to today, thanks to the likes of AI and search engines – it was not impossible so we cannot know how much assistance from friends and relatives they may have had. The prize was usually monetary, but other prizes ranged from knives, to sewing kits to a grand piano.

Other competitions include literary based and naming contests. Lotteries also pre-date newspapers and news on where to buy lottery tickets and names of winners can be frequently found. A winner's name, occupation and residence may be provided. One example in *The Kentish Gazette* on 28 March 1786 names James Parkinson Esq. as the winner of Sir Ashton Lever's Lottery. James is stated to be a law stationer from Castle Yard in Holborn.

Other

The subjects featured in a newspaper are unlimited and you may therefore find a type of article naming your ancestor that is not featured here. It is often these more miscellaneous reports that can provide the most interest to the reader, often about a person who has done something outlandish or peculiar. People were featured for being hoarders or hermits, named as a human exhibit in a 'freak show', reported for having physical deformities or disappearing without a trace. They may be recorded as having unexplained physical or mental health symptoms, which we may now be able to diagnose thanks to advanced medical science and understanding. Early newspapers were not bound by the same privacy laws as they are today so there is much evidence of gossip entered as a story. This could be about a street dispute, a scandalous romantic liaison or comments on a person's difference of character. There are cryptic placements in the eighteenth century of challenges to duels. You may be very surprised as to what you discover about your family tree through newspaper records.

Royalty has always featured regularly in newspapers. For those of you with royal ancestors, you will often have the opposite problem to those of us who do not in that you will have too many articles to choose from! Most early reports are the same, simply copied and pasted from one title to another. While the British royal family still features heavily in the press, stories of foreign royal families feature much less frequently than they used to. If you are tracing a line relating to a royal family from overseas, you will likely find a multitude of articles in the eighteenth and early nineteenth centuries regarding their movements around Europe, their births, marriage and deaths and attendance at various occasions. Today, this is usually only reported if there is a notable scandal. It is much the same for the more distant British royal family members.

Fiction and poetry have featured regularly in newspapers since the eighteenth century. Reading the language and subject can help us contextualise our ancestor's life and what literary text was like at their time. Newspapers often published entire books in daily or weekly instalments which helped encourage readers to keep purchasing their newspaper. If your ancestor was an author they may be named, and it was common for authors, including Charles Dickens and Thomas

A humorous cartoon depicting the 'latest modern horror' of the pocket telephone as seen in *The Daily Mirror* on 5 March 1919. *(Supplied by British Cartoon Archive, University of Kent)*

Hardy, to publish their stories this way. Fiction like this is rarely found published in newspapers in this manner today, with excerpts often being favoured instead to encourage readers to purchase the book rather than multiple copies of a newspaper.

There are columns, or sometimes multiple pages, dedicated to certain lifestyle features including cookery, fashion and gardening. Some had sections aimed at women and children. These can all be of relevance to us to various degrees. If your ancestor was a gardener, you may wish to read the gardening section to read the latest tips or what tools of the trade were being used. You will come across advertisements and reviews of new publications, paintings and films. If you are aware your ancestor was interested in reading, art or film this will be of particular interest to you.

You can also choose to view the public opinion on any topic, such as long engagements, the introduction of formula feeding, mixed race marriages and divorce, among a huge number of other examples. If there are certain topics that you know were relevant to your forebear's life, it is worth exploring. There are also humorous examples relating to views on the latest inventions and thoughts on possible future technology. The example on the previous page is a cartoon from *The Daily Mirror* on 5 March 1919, demonstrating how disastrous and inconvenient a mobile phone would be.

Chapter 12

USING NEWSPAPERS AS A GENEALOGICAL SOURCE

Newspapers are a genealogical source in their own right, although, as has been stressed, corroborating evidence should always be sought where possible. You can use reports to find dates of birth, baptism, marriage, death and burial, as well as names of family members. These family ties could be anyone from parents, children and siblings to grandparents, cousins and aunts and uncles. Neighbours, friends and colleagues may also be named, as well as names of ministers telling you what chapel they attended. Family may be named in any type of article. This could include court reports, articles surrounding accidents, in sports pages and in passenger lists, among many others. This means your ancestor may also be named in articles about their more distant family. Therefore, as well as searching for articles surrounding your direct lineage, look for reports naming first and second cousins to see if your ancestor is mentioned. This is especially the case where a distant cousin or other relative's name is given in full but your ancestor is only given by their surname or other identifying feature, such as the nature of their relationship, e.g. Charlotte Williamson's uncle, Mr Smith.

When we are viewing historical newspapers, there are important issues to be aware of. These largely surround bias, misinterpretation and the language of the past. In order to make sure we understand the context of the material we are reading and have a good idea of how reliable the information is, the following information is crucial.

Reliability

When we are using newspaper articles to further our genealogical research, we must consider the reason for its publication and its original source. Newspapers have never been, and are still not, completely reliable in the information that they provide. Much of the reporting is politically biased or exaggerated. Where verbatim reports are given in court, we must consider whether what the person is saying is true.

There are a wide number of cases that have been reported on that have now been established as false. One example is the Parnell Commission where, in 1888, *The Times* published letters supposedly written by Irish politician Charles Stewart Parnell condoning violence and murder. The letters were later proven to be forgeries. Multiple newspapers printed false stories regarding the health of King George II in the mid-1700s and *The Sunday Times* published what it believed to be excerpts from Hitler's Diary in 1983, but this was again a forgery.

Aside from forgeries, many stories are unreliable due to the pressure on journalists to publish stories quickly. This resulted in inaccurate articles from a lack of source checking. Today, newspapers are often forced to issue corrections and apologies for major errors, but this has not always been the case. Always try to find a corroborating source where possible to back up claims found in an article.

Certain sections of society have historically not had their voices heard. You may find it harder to research the views of women, ethnic minorities, the disabled and the poor when using newspapers as a source. As researchers, we can learn a lot about what is omitted from newspapers. This may be due to purposeful censorship or down to an editorial decision. Whatever the reasoning, bear in mind that a lack of representation from a certain group within society when discussing a social issue can lead to biased reporting and makes an article a less reliable and a less comprehensive source.

As with much genealogical documentation, the difference in the date that the article is written and the date that the event occurred should be noted. If the article is about an event that occurred on the same day and was rushed to print in an evening newspaper title then it is more likely to contain some factual errors. These may become more apparent over the following days if the story is covered at a later date, after journalists had time to check their facts. There is also the issue that if the article relates to something that happened several years or decades prior then inaccuracies may have crept in. This is most commonly seen in the case of reminiscence articles where people's memories are quoted and may be misremembered. This may feature in an obituary, an article about a couple's golden wedding anniversary or a witness to a large-scale event recalling the occasion differently after many years have passed. Again, corroboration here is key.

Language

When researching old newspapers, it is important to remember the time that they were written. Language used in the past that was previously acceptable has now often changed meaning and is now unacceptable. There are a wide variety of examples that can be used here, some more offensive today than others.

One example you are likely to have come across before are the terms idiot, imbecile and lunatic. These are used in some of the early census returns. If we were asked the same question today with the same terminology, i.e. 'How many lunatics are there in your household?', respondents would rightfully be upset by the question. All three terms have changed their meaning over time and at the time the censuses were compiled these were not derogatory words. Idiots and imbeciles usually refer to those who had learning difficulties or were neurodivergent, whereas lunatics refer to people who were severely mentally ill.

These terms commonly appear in newspapers. Some vocabulary can be shocking to read. As researchers we need to remember the time that they were written and understand the meaning may have changed. Try to extract any fact from such an article that you can. If an ancestor is referred to as a lunatic, you can then try to find any surviving documentation of a possible stay in their local mental health facility, again probably known as a lunatic asylum.

As well as offensive language, you may come across some words, idioms and metaphors that are now rarely used or obsolete. In these cases, use a search engine to discover their meaning. This will ensure you fully understand the article you are reading. This is more common with newspapers from the early eighteenth century or earlier news sheets. It is often the case that the word may be the same but is spelt differently today.

Controversy of Historical Events

Newspapers are a fantastic source for researching how historical events were reported at the time. There is no limit as to what you can research; from wars to medical breakthroughs to the deaths of public figures and the changing of laws, we can choose to look up any topic we like. When doing so, we must remember the circumstances in which they were written. Where there is a general opinion given towards a topic in newspapers, we should also not assume our ancestors would have agreed with this.

The slave trade in Britain was not abolished until 1807 and not abolished in the rest of the British Empire until 1833. As this is well into the time when newspapers were being published, we can read reports about slavery at a time when it was still legal in Britain. A harrowing read in *The Derby Mercury* on 6 October 1791 gives us insight as to how the treatment of slaves abroad was being reported in Britain. The report tells us slaves in the West Indies are 'considered as a species of inferior beings' by their owners. There is much insight into the living conditions as it continues: 'The field slave work in rows, under the whip of drivers, which hurries many to the grave', 'their little huts are built by themselves with poles and thatched at the top and sides with a kind of bamboo', 'some slept on the ground and others on a board raised from it'. Describing punishment through mutilation of one particular slave, the report notes: 'no more notice was taken of clipping off the ears of a female slave than if a dog's ears had been cut off'.

If you are researching an ancestor who was enslaved, it is worth researching about their living conditions to discover what they endured. As you would expect, the slaves themselves are very rarely named. If you are researching slavery as a general topic to gain historical context of your ancestor's time, be aware they may not have agreed with slavery because it was legal.

If you think of certain laws which have changed in our lifetimes, we will not agree with something simply because it was legal or disagree with it because it was illegal. For example, many people disagreed with hunting before it was banished and others agreed with euthanasia despite its illegality. There are numerous topics, including homosexuality, abortion and the strengthening of gun control, which can all be used as examples of laws that have changed in the last 100 years. We cannot assume that our ancestors agreed with the law of their time without evidence to the contrary.

We must also remember that historical events and political issues are reported accordingly to the stance and beliefs of the newspaper title. How certain topics are discussed will vary from one title to the next depending on their political suasion. Therefore, if you are researching historical views from a certain period, it is wise to read as many differing titles as possible to gain an unbiased overview.

False Impressions

We should remember that newspapers wish to sell copies and to do so the stories must at least be interesting and at most be outrageous or scandalous. As a result, newspapers generally fail to give a fair impression of what life was really like at the time. This remains true today. Stories of negative topics such as crime feature heavily. Lighthearted, comedic or positive stories tend not to sell as well, so often take a back seat. There are exceptions, such as royal weddings, but largely the front pages will feature a more negative story. Even today when we read the newspapers, we must remember that serious criminals make up a tiny proportion of the British population. Because we read about them every day, this proportion is exacerbated; this is also true in the past. It is the reason why we may often feel depressed about the state of the world after we have read the news today. Reading newspaper stories from hundreds of years ago can help us to compare these with those from today.

As well as gaining a false impression of the state of the country or world overall, reading newspaper articles can often give us an unfair idea of our ancestors. If a particular ancestor only features in two articles, both in which he is described as being drunk and disorderly, this does not necessarily mean he was like this for a long period. He may have been a trustworthy, upstanding man who simply went through a short rough patch. Be careful not to assume the character of an ancestor from such limited information. In cases of repeat offenders, it is hard to discover their good qualities. Alternatively, if there are a handful of articles highlighting an ancestor's charity work this does not mean they had no bad qualities. Take the information that you have and ensure you judge it fairly.

Using Corroborative Sources

It cannot be emphasised enough that newspapers are one of a huge range of potential genealogical sources. There are occasions where an article will be the only evidence that remains of a particular event in our ancestor's life. However, in most cases there will be corroborating evidence and we should ensure that this is uncovered. Not only will finding additional sources help us to prove that an article relates to our ancestor, they could also add extra information to what the newspaper article tells us.

For some stories, it will be easy to find a corroborating source. This may be a certificate of civil registration or an entry in a parish register to confirm details within a births, marriages and deaths column. It could also involve requesting court records, military records, passenger lists or school registers. A mention of an ancestor in a business advertisement, playing with a named sports team, or as a member of a particular club may help you to discover related records held by local archives.

Where you find your ancestor named, try and think what other records exist that can help you corroborate the facts written in the article

This image shows four generations of one family, in *The Berwick Journal* on 15 October 1915. They are named as great-grandmother Sarah Chirnside, her son-in-law Robert Dalgetty, his daughter Margaret Craig and Sarah's great grandson Peter Logan Craig. Four or more living generations in one family was enough to provide interest to readers of provincial newspapers. Their relationship to each other should be checked with other sources. *(Content provided by the British Library Board. All rights reserved. With thanks to The British Newspaper Archive (www.britishnewspaperarchive.co.uk))*

and what sources could help you add to the information. Reading about more generic details, such as a natural disaster in your ancestor's parish, may encourage you to read more about the history of the area in local history books. At other times, newspaper articles may actually be the corroborating source. If you are unsure whether you have the right death certificate for somebody who is noted to have had a coroner's inquest, it is likely that the inquest records will not survive. A newspaper article about the inquest usually provides much more detail than a death certificate and should be enough to confirm identification. You may also have a named photograph of a person in your family ephemera and be unsure who they are, only to find a relative announced their engagement in the local newspaper only to have never married.

This book focuses on newspaper articles but it is very much encouraged to read about further sources. By reading into the subject of genealogy, you can learn what sources survive for each instance that relates to your ancestor, discover what information they contain and the dates for which they survive. Ensure you never rely on what is available on the internet as county archives hold a vast array of useful documentation. Only a small percentage of this is available online and this archived material may hold the key to breaking down a brick wall or discovering more about a forebear.

Chapter 13

HOW TO FIND RELEVANT NEWSPAPER ARTICLES

In some cases, you may be lucky and typing in your ancestor's name into one of the websites named in Chapter 14 brings up an instant result. Even in these cases we need to be careful that we are researching the right person. You may be surprised to find that your ancestor with a fairly uncommon name has a namesake residing in the same area. This is especially the case where articles do not give a person's full name, instead listing them as Mr Taylor or Mr A. Taylor. Here we will look at the different variations of a person's name needed to do a thorough search, different terms you can search for, using wildcards to widen your search and different options available to use online.

Some genealogy websites, such as Ancestry, have introduced using Artificial Intelligence (AI) to generate automatic hints from newspapers. Therefore, if you have your family tree saved on a particular website, you may be able to find articles quickly and easily this way. Be aware that any suggested hint will not necessarily be correct and will need checking to ensure it relates to your ancestor. Never rely on this function solely to find records, as a huge number will be missed by AI. This service will also only search the newspaper titles that are held by that company, rather than an exhaustive search across all databases.

Naturally, we want to discover as much about our ancestors' appearances in the media as we can. There is no right order to do so, with many people starting by researching with their grandparents and working backwards to their great-grandparents and beyond. Remember that contemporary newspapers are also available to search, meaning your parents and siblings may also be found. As mentioned previously, please do this sensitively and with care and respect to living relatives.

Remember to research your own name – you may be surprised to discover your name in a newspaper article that you previously were not aware had been published.

How to Search for Names

An issue when searching by an ancestor's name is that it may not always be presented in a predictable way. For example, Arthur Charles Keep may appear under his full name. He may also appear under Arthur C. Keep, A.C. Keep, A. Charles Keep, Charles Keep or Mr Keep. His wife may appear as Mrs Keep or Mrs Arthur Keep, rather than by her own first name. This means for each person, you will need to conduct a number of searches to make sure you have found all the relevant articles. If you are searching for a married female ancestor it is always worth searching for her husband's name in case hers is not recorded. Remember the date that they married as a woman will appear under her maiden name before her marriage. Sometimes, women also appear under their maiden name after marriage. This is more common in Scottish newspapers, or if the person is recorded as 'Mrs John Rowland, formerly Miss Mary Holbourn', the latter example more common among the upper classes. Search also for any aliases or nicknames your ancestor went by, including if they were usually recorded by their middle name first, as this may help you discover more articles. Similarly, a name may be shortened as we frequently see in other genealogical records, such as Thos. for Thomas, and Eliz. For Elizabeth.

The example above of Arthur Charles Keep also presents another problem. 'Keep' is a common noun and when searching for names such as this you will find that a wide range of articles are suggested for you with the word keep rather than the name. There is, unfortunately, little you can do in this case as OCR is not able to recognise what is a name and what is not. The best option you have is to place the name in quotation marks, i.e. "Arthur Charles Keep" as this should search for the exact phrase as you have given it. You will have to repeat this with each name variant to find all possible results.

As odd as it may sound, you may have luck if you purposefully misspell your ancestor's name for a search. Many letters in print are frequently confused by OCR. These include 'y' and 'g', and 'h' and 'b'. With this in mind, think how your ancestor's name may be misread by a computer. The name 'Hatcher' may be transcribed as 'Hatcber' and the name 'Legg' may be read as 'Leyy'. It is worth spending time trying some alternatives.

The spelling of names has only been standardised in recent times, so you may find your ancestor under a spelling variation. This could be 'Smyth' instead of 'Smith' or 'Burnill' instead of 'Burnal'. The spelling will depend on where the journalist or editor heard the name. This may have been in print directly from your ancestors, which increases the likelihood of an accurate spelling, or it may have been through word of mouth. For this reason, you will need to try different variations in spelling of your ancestor's surname, and sometimes forenames too, if these are less common.

As with many genealogical records, it is recommended to search for other relatives of your direct ancestors to see if you get any results. This is not only to see if they themselves got up to anything newsworthy, but also to see if your direct ancestor is named. My third great-grandmother Mary Jane Taylor has a very common name which is hard to filter to find correct results. By searching for her granddaughter's rarer name of Maud Costello, this brought up a match showing that Mary was called to court to give evidence against her daughter-in-law for neglecting Maud.

If your ancestor had a title other than Mr or Mrs remember this is an important term to search for. This may be Rev., P.C., Dr or Earl, among many other examples. This is especially true when researching military ancestors whose first names were often not supplied. Colonel John Grainger may therefore appear as Col. Grainger. There are again some anomalies to bear in mind here. My husband's ancestor was named Baron Gerard. He had no title, with Baron being his given name. When searching for Baron Gerard, however, results bring up titled individuals. Always be careful to check the article is referring to your ancestor.

Some search engines have separate search boxes for 'name' and 'keyword', such as on the British Newspaper Archive and Findmypast. It is worth searching for people's names in both as the 'name' feature can remove relevant articles. At the time of writing, using Findmypast's newspaper search function for my own name I get fifteen results when this is placed into the 'name' box and 2,243 results when it is placed into the keyword box. The latter will show you more results from where the two words are not placed directly next to each other. These are often still relevant to the named person. An article may begin by writing about 'Mrs O'Shea' before naming her as 'Chloe' later on, for example. This will also cover where part of a full name is translated incorrectly by OCR but the other part is correctly deciphered later on in the article.

Some websites claim that by placing the name in the 'name' box rather than the 'keyword' box can help find those tricky names like Keep as mentioned earlier. This is still not entirely reliable though, so it is worth checking both where possible as some relevant records may be omitted.

Historically, there was a convention among writers to partly anonymise names by placing dashes within them. This was usually only if the person was not supposed to be easily identified, such as a person writing a letter who wished to remain largely anonymous or if particular prostitutes were being discussed. Dashes were sometimes placed in the middle of a name leaving only the beginning and end letter, such as 'Mrs M------l' instead of Mrs Marshall, and at other times the vowels were all replaced with a dash, such as 'Mrs M-rsh-ll'. This is most commonly found in the eighteenth century and newspaper databases struggle to find these records currently. This may improve in time with new developments in OCR and automatic search functions, but for now it means these articles are difficult to find without browsing. In many cases, names written in this manner are often aliases.

Other Terms to Research

There are times where our ancestor may feature in an article but not by their name. These can be the hardest reports to find. Occasionally there will be an article stating for example 'a boy aged six of 24 Oak Road was hit by a car' or 'the postman of Longton was involved in an altercation.' These examples show the importance of searching for terms other than a person's name. There is usually, but not always, some identifying information supplied. This can be a person's address or occupation as seen previously. I have had particular success when searching for my ancestors' addresses. These can be found in documents, such as census returns, title deeds, civil registration certificates of birth, marriage and death, as well as criminal records. Our ancestors moved frequently, so try searching for each address within the date range they may have lived there. For example, if they are living in different addresses in the 1901, 1911 and 1921 census returns you can search for the address in the 1911 census with a date range of 1901–1920 to see if you get any results. This is also a useful technique if you are tracing a house history.

As well as searching for your ancestor's specific address, try searching for their parish of residence to see what was happening in the area that they lived when they resided there. The aim of this is not to find articles that specifically discuss your ancestor, but rather to gain an idea of their surroundings and any events that have occurred in their locality. Depending on where your ancestor lived this could be the name of a village, town or a particular area of a city. Topics may include local crime, accidents and natural disasters. There may also be cheerier topics such as fundraisers, village meet-ups and local improvement schemes. If you have a long line of ancestors residing in a parish try searching using the name of the parish along with the surname. This can result in many family members being shown in the results. Be aware also that the names of parishes have changed over time and some are simply misspelt in newspapers in the same way as names may be. Examples from my own tree include Sutton Pointz instead of Sutton Poyntz; Eddlesborough instead of Edlesborough; and Sympson instead of Simpson.

Including the name of a county tends not to work as well in provincial newspapers when looking for specific people, as most of the news in later times will largely relate to the relevant county anyway so there is no need for it to be included in the article. For example, you are more likely to have a successful search with 'William White, Sarre', than 'William White, Kent' in local articles. If news reached a national publication, the county is more likely to be included, but not always.

Searching for a person's occupation can be trickier to find specific people. In some cases where names are also given, occupations can help with positive identification. If there are two Andrew Adams living in the same town but you know they have different occupations, this can help you discover which article relates to your ancestor. If the occupation was a less common one, such as a postmaster of a named town or a reverend, these can be used as search terms in their own right along with their parish, with no name needed. Alternatively, you may wish to search by their occupation alone to gain a general idea of what this was like at the time. You may find articles referring to the occupation being in decline, or as being dangerous with a number of fatalities, or sometimes even a description of what a person's working day involved. If you are using two search terms, it usually works best to place a comma between the two, such as 'postmaster, Longdon'.

If you are searching for an article about a specific event that you already know the date of, such as a death or an accident, you can try searching using the date filters. Try narrowing down the newspapers to the county the event occurred in and then narrow the date first to the week of the event, and then the following week. News could sometimes be reported on the same day it occurred in the evening newspaper or alternatively it could take a few weeks to reach the press. You may wish to add a generic relevant term such as 'deaths' if searching for a notice in the deaths column. This will help to discover articles that either do not give your ancestor's name or where it has not been transcribed correctly by OCR.

You may also choose to search for an event that you know your ancestor was involved in to read the journalist's report. This could be anything from a battle to a Christmas lights switch on. The type of event will determine whether to search in national newspapers, local press or both. For example, a church fundraiser will only appear in local press, whereas battles of a world war will feature in the national news. Battles may have been given the names we know them by now long after the event took place, so as well as this title try searching for the location that the battle took place.

Try searching for anything you know about your ancestor that may have been newsworthy. My grandmother was a member of her local WI group and there are numerous articles in the local newspaper about what they had been up to, including noting that she had won a limerick competition. Try searches to include political groups and charities that your ancestor supported or was a member of. You may wish to research a topic whose known term has changed over time; for example, pugilism instead of boxing, motor vehicle instead of car or nursing instead of breastfeeding. Abbreviations are also found in these other search terms as they are for names. Examples include 'Rd' instead of Road, 'Northants' for Northamptonshire, 'JP' for Justice of the Peace and 'Corp' for Corporation.

Wildcards

A person's name could either be spelt incorrectly in a newspaper article or have been transcribed incorrectly by OCR. This is where wildcards can be very useful when searching newspapers online. Wildcards are symbols used in place of letters and can save you time searching for endless spelling variants. The spelling of a person's name was only standardised in recent times with the increase in education. Today, your name is spelt the same in all of your official documents for identification purposes. In our ancestor's day this was less important to them. A journalist may be writing an article about a person whose name they have heard but not seen written down. It would therefore be their decision as to how to spell it. Even our ancestors themselves were often illiterate and unaware of how to spell their own names.

You will need to think of all the possible spelling variants when searching for your ancestor, both online and when viewing documentation in person. This may apply to both their first name and surname, as well as any middle names. Having a lack of understanding of spelling variations and surname changes is a very common cause of having a brick wall in your tree. Your ancestor may appear in newspaper articles in the same year with the different surname of 'Richard' and 'Richards', 'Wilson' and 'Willson' or 'Tomson' and 'Thompson', for example. Using wildcard options when searching online newspaper databases can return a wider diversity of search results. From here you can decide if they are relevant to your ancestor or not.

The first wildcard is '?' which can replace a single letter in a person's name meaning searching for 'B?ll' will return results relating to Ball, Bell and Bull, among others. The second wildcard is '*' which will match with more than one character. For example, searching for 'Davids*' will give results for Davids and Davidson, as well as any other names that have been transcribed as starting with those letters.

By using a wildcard, you may find an erroneous transcription relating to your ancestor. Try searching on different websites where possible. Some newspapers have been digitised by more than one company, meaning one of their OCR techniques may have read the name correctly whereas another has not. Wildcards can of course be used with any term, not just names. If you are searching for a place name or occupation, for example, it is worth using wildcards in case of a spelling or transcription error. Transcription errors can be difficult, if not somewhat impossible, to combat. The surname 'Fletcher' could end up being transcribed as 'F1ele0oi-' for example. This is more commonly seen in older newspapers where the letters are bolder and harder for computers to read automatically, or where the digitisation process has left the text with a very faint appearance. In cases such as these, wildcards are not of as much use and you may need to browse the newspaper page by page. Wildcards work well where accents, umlauts and other special characters have been used in the text that OCR has not recognised, such as é, ë and ç. For example, if an ancestor is named Chloe but is sometimes referred to as Chloé and you are not sure how OCR will interpret the text, you can search for 'Chlo?' to cover all bases.

Not all websites allow the use of wildcards. At the time of writing, Findmypast, for example, allows wildcard searches in its main records section but this does not work well in its newspaper search facility. Newspapers.com by Ancestry does allow wildcards. For each site, try using wildcards to see what result you get. Remember that some newspaper titles are duplicated on various websites so you may want to search via one that allows wildcards to get the results you need.

Browsing Newspapers

There may be times when it is beneficial to you to browse historical newspapers page by page. This is obviously very time-consuming; however, it does have its benefits. If you find an article about an ancestor in a newspaper, you may wish to read other articles from the same issue to see what else was happening in the local area at the time. This can provide a very useful historical context. For example, if your ancestor is named in the births column you can see what products were advertised when they were born, how much they cost, any recent weather events and what concerns from local residents were in the letters' pages.

If you believe that your ancestor should feature in the local newspaper but cannot find a story via the usual searching methods you may wish to browse page by page. This is not always as time-consuming as you may expect, as newspapers tend to be laid out in the same way with clear headlines, particularly the more recent editions. For example, if you know your ancestor appeared in court on a particular date you may wish to search the 'In the courts' section for the days following the event. Similarly, if you know the date that they died you may wish to browse the deaths column for the following two weeks to see if they feature. When you successfully find a relevant article, you may find that the page is damaged or that the scan is faulty, informing you why the OCR search was unsuccessful.

Online Techniques and Options

There are many different websites you can use to search for newspaper articles and all have different search features and filters. Some of these will be discussed in the next chapter. Most will allow you to filter results by date, county and publication title. Be careful not to filter results too heavily as you are at risk of eliminating relevant results. There are numerous examples of people featuring in the newspapers many years after their deaths, and stories which only appear in counties other than where they lived. In Memoriams, for example, were often published annually many years after a person's death. Try to use a common-sense approach when searching. You can be sure that a person cannot feature in a newspaper before their birth so you automatically have a solid year to start searching from. Begin by entering your search term to see how many results there are. If there are too many to reasonably look through, you can begin filtering them as is best appropriate.

The best example I can give for the above relates to my fourth great-grandfather William Read (1781–1847). Just using the usual genealogical documentation paints William as having a rather ordinary life as an agricultural labourer in Sutton Poyntz and neighbouring Preston in Dorset. He married Mary Croad in 1816 at the age of 35, which was certainly older than average for the time for a first marriage. He did not appear in any records between his baptism and marriage, which raised some questions as to his whereabouts in these missing years. It was an article in *The Western Gazette* on 6 April 1934, nearly ninety years after William's death, that solved the mystery. The report is actually an obituary for his grandson Charles Osment which details some of William's history, albeit not by name. Instead, William is referred to as Charles's 'grandfather on his mother's side' and it is noted that he 'was interned in a French prison for 21 years during the wars with France'. The account is obviously second (or even third) hand and the true number of years may be slightly out, but this detail explains William's absence from records and his late marriage. This highlights not only the fact that you often need to be flexible with dates after a known event or a person's death, but also the fact that searching by an ancestor's name alone is not enough. Searching for 'William Read' would not bring up this result as he was not named in the obituary. Therefore, ensure you search for more distant relatives as well as those on your direct line. In this example, the Osment family had a long history of residing in Sutton Poyntz so to cover a lot of bases I searched for 'Osment, Poyntz' which uncovered this result.

Some websites, such as the British Newspaper Archive, allow you to exclude certain words from your results using their advanced search feature. This can be useful to discard articles you know will be irrelevant to you. You may also opt to choose to search a term using the exact wording by selecting the tick box if there is one of placing a term in quotation marks. This means searching for "Boer War" will search for that exact phrasing, rather than articles that mention words singularly. This works well in many cases where you would expect the exact wording to be used, but be careful of the time frame within which you are searching. The First World War, for example, was referred to as The Great War prior to the Second World War. Many sites also have the option to filter by article type, such as advertisement, family notice and images. This is not a foolproof option, however, so do not rely on it too heavily.

As many websites are updated frequently, it can help to sort your results by their most recently added date. This is especially the case if you have a family member you regularly research. My aforementioned second great-grandfather Alexander Taylor featured very frequently in the local press for his criminal activities. It is useful for me to be able to search for his name with the most recently added results viewable at the top to save time going through the previously viewed results first. Most websites will show a 'tick' in the corner of the image result to show you have already viewed the page.

Newspapers needed to fit as much information on to the page as possible. The printers therefore used hyphenated words frequently at the end of a line to break a long word into two short words. This is not always in a logical place, such as 'part-time' or 'left-handed', and can be anywhere in the word, including names, such as 'William-son', 'Williamson' or 'Wil-liamson'. This can make searching for these terms very difficult. You can try searching for the beginning of a word followed by the '*' wildcard, or alternatively use the wildcard at the beginning if searching for the second part of a word. This is likely to result in a large number of unrelated terms, however.

Text in earlier newspapers often appears different and may appear unfamiliar to less experienced researchers. The best example of this is the old letter 's' which is often interpreted by OCR (as well as some manual transcribers) to be a letter 'f'. The name 'Williamson' may therefore be read as 'Williamfon'. This will again apply to all terms, not just names. Therefore, when searching for a name or term in the eighteenth and early nineteenth centuries, try swapping the letter 's' for an 'f' to see what results you obtain.

As well as the aforementioned wildcards, you can also use various search operators to discover more relevant results. These include using 'AND', 'OR' and 'NOT' in your search box and can be very useful. AND will ensure two search terms are both included in the results (Blundell AND Baptist), OR will give results of two terms but not featured together (Squibb OR blacksmith) and NOT will omit results with a term featured after the word (Pinney NOT mariner). You can also choose to use more than one parameter in each search, such as Alexander AND Maidstone NOT stonemason. These parameters work with varying degrees according to each website and are worth playing around with. I find the NOT function particularly useful to instantly eliminate irrelevant results, such as a person with the same name as an ancestor but with a different occupation or place of residence, without the need to scroll through them.

Some databases, such as the British Newspaper Archive, automatically include certain spelling variants in their search results, such as Baptist and Baptiste. This can be extremely useful in saving you time trying various search terms so make sure you are paying attention to the results so you know which variants you do not need to search for separately on that database. This feature can, however, also be slightly annoying if it is not relevant. In the previous example, it may be useful if you are searching for a person with the surname of Baptist who may also be found under the variant of Baptiste; however, if you are searching for a person of the Baptist faith you are likely to uncover irrelevant results. This is where the NOT function can come in useful. Most searches are not case sensitive, so you should receive the same results whether you search for 'Wilson' or wilson.

As the use of AI is increasing, newspaper websites are beginning to explore how this can be used to the benefit of their users. In November 2025, Findmypast launched its 'AI Newspaper Search' service. At the time of writing, this allows users to ask a question which AI will then answer by browsing the contents of four historic newspapers from 1910 to 1949. This can help us to find out about public opinion on certain matters, as well as more specific queries. This is a feature that is likely to be further expanded in the future.

Also on Findmypast is a page dedicated to specific topics it refers to as 'Collections', which can be found at https://www.findmypast.co.uk/collections. Subjects of interest, such as 'Faces of the Fallen: First World War memorials' and 'The Wartime Women of WW1' can be browsed easily using its selected newspaper extracts. This is a great way of browsing about a particular topic, rather than searching for a named person.

Reading Newspapers Offline

You may prefer to view newspapers via a more traditional method. Before digitisation, of course, this was the only way. Many libraries, archives and museums still retain historical newspapers, some of which are not yet available online. Some of these services previously created indexes for newspaper articles. This is usually of people's names but may also be places. This can be a useful method of searching for someone, particularly where transcription errors have occurred online or where the newspaper title has not yet been digitised. It is worth checking with the local facilities to see if they have any indexes to newspapers available.

If you wish to view a newspaper in an archive or library you will almost always be asked to view them on microfilm. This involves using a machine to view scanned images of the newspaper page by page. Check online before you visit to make sure they have the newspaper title you wish to see for the dates you wish to peruse.

Archives also sometimes have scrapbooks of newspaper clippings which have been handed in to them. This may have been created by a person logging articles relating to their family, collecting articles about a particular event or war or sometimes even a pastime such as trains or equestrian sports. A scrapbook such as this which is useful to you may not always be found in the correct county archive so try searching via TNA Discovery page at **https://discovery.nationalarchives.gov.uk** to see if there are any positive results.

You may also, of course, have physical copies of newspapers or clippings handed down to you or a cousin within the family. Try reaching out to family members to see what has survived. These clippings often have the newspaper title and date cut off.

Saving your Research

When you have found an article relating to your family history, you may wonder about the best way to save this information to your tree. This can be down to personal choice or other issues, such as the size of the article or where you found it. If you have found the article in a library or archive via microfilm you can pay to print a copy for your files. You may then choose to scan this in at home to save to your online tree. In this case, be careful of copyright issues.

If you are uploading copyrighted images to an online tree, then your tree should be kept private to avoid flouting copyright law. This is the same with any copyrighted document, not just newspaper articles, and applies whether you found the image online or not. You can save images found on Ancestry to an online public tree on its website, and the same for Findmypast where images found via its search facility can be saved on an online tree on its site. If you keep your family tree saved via a software program that is only viewable to you then the images can be safely and legally uploaded there.

When wishing to save an article you can either choose to 'print screen', then crop and save the image to your hard drive or you may wish to crop the article using the website's own features where applicable. There is a 'Clip' feature on both Findmypast and Ancestry's Newspapers.com and some sites also have an option to save the entire page as a PDF file. When you save an image to your tree, ensure you have also saved the image to your hard drive separately. No website is guaranteed to save your data forever so it is important to back up our research on our own home devices in case a company folds or is hacked resulting in data loss. The general advice with any digital data is to back it up in more than one place. This may be via separate hard drives for example, in case one of them fails. You may also choose to print newspaper articles so you have a paper copy.

How you crop an article is your choice. If your ancestor features in a births, marriages and deaths column you may choose to simply crop out the two or three lines that refer to them or you may choose to crop the column back up to the title. If your ancestor featured as a witness in a court case that is a particularly lengthy feature you may choose to crop only what is relevant to your ancestor or you may wish to save the entire article for context.

However you choose to crop and save your newspaper articles, make sure you have recorded the title of the newspaper, the date it was published and the page it is found on. There are options to do this when saving images to online and offline trees. Always ensure any documents or images are sourced. This way you can refer to them again if needed and you can also see where you have already researched to avoid repeating a search in the future. Check the image after you have saved it to make sure it is of a readable quality.

Case Study

Searching for one ancestor alone in newspaper records is time-consuming. There are a wide range of spelling variations for every name, address, occupation or other term that should be used in case of a transcription error. They may have had multiple occupations over the years that need researching, or lived in many different parishes. The more siblings and children they had, the more relatives that will also need researching in case your focus ancestor is mentioned within it because either OCR has not picked it up or they are not identified by name. The table below shows a condensed timeline for my great-grandfather William Eggelton simply using civil registration records, census returns and military records. Further genealogical records can be used to gather more search terms. Following this timeline is a list of potential search terms that could be used to discover more about William's life in newspapers. This may give you some ideas on how to uncover stories about ancestors you are struggling to find within newspaper search databases.

Date (Age)	Event	Location	Source	Other Details
11th Sep 1885 (0)	Birth	Linslade, Buckinghamshire	Birth certificate	Parents Robert and Kate Eggelton
15th Mar 1888 (2)	Death of mother	Linslade, Buckinghamshire	Death certificate	Father Robert a railway labourer
5th Apr 1891 (5)	Census	Linslade, Buckinghamshire	1891 census	Scholar living with father Robert and Aunt Jane Vickers
31st Mar 1901 (15)	Census	46 Park Street, Fenny Stratford, Buckinghamshire	1901 census	Painter's Labourer living with father Robert, sister Ada and stepmother Clara
2 April 1911 (25)	Census	13 South Terrace, Bletchley, Buckinghamshire	1911 census	Working for 'Railway Company', single. Living with father Robert, stepmother Clara and cousin Frederick Vickers
19 Feb 1912 (26)	Marriage	13 South Terrace, Bletchley, Buckinghamshire	Marriage certificate	Carpenter. Married 26-year-old Sophia Bowler at Fenny Stratford parish church
1 Jun 1912 (26)	Son Arthur born	35 Victoria Road, Fenny Stratford, Buckinghamshire	Birth certificate	William a 'Carpenter on railway'

(Cont'd)

Date (Age)	Event	Location	Source	Other Details
29 Dec 1913 (28)	Son Frederick born	35 Victoria Road, Fenny Stratford, Buckinghamshire	Birth certificate	William a 'Carpenter on railway'
1914–1918 (28–33)	Military Service	Served in France	Military records (award rolls, medal index cards, oral history)	Served as a private with the Oxford and Buckinghamshire Light Infantry (203194), Royal Welsh Fusiliers (235070) and Machine Gun Corps (152360)
9 Apr 1920 (34)	Son Robert born	35 Victoria Road, Fenny Stratford, Buckinghamshire	Birth certificate	William a 'Carpenter on railway'
19 Jun 1921 (35)	Census	35 Victoria Road, Fenny Stratford, Buckinghamshire	1921 census	Railway Carpenter for L + N.W. Railway Co. Living with wife Sophia and their three sons
1 Mar 1922 (36)	Daughter Clara born	35 Victoria Road, Fenny Stratford, Buckinghamshire	Birth certificate	William a 'Carpenter on railway'
28 Oct 1934 (49)	Death of father	13 South Terrace, Bletchley, Buckinghamshire	Death certificate	William's stepmother Clara the informant. Father Robert listed as 'carpenter on railway'
29 Sep 1939 (54)	National Registration Act	35 Victoria Road, Fenny Stratford, Buckinghamshire	1939 Register	Carpenter for LMS Railway. Living with wife Sophia, son Robert and daughter Clara
20 April 1951 (65)	Death	35 Victoria Road, Fenny Stratford, Buckinghamshire	Death certificate	Retired railway carpenter. Son Frederick the informant. Cause of death given as cancer of the stomach

Timeline for William Eggelton

Using the above extracted facts from William's life, we can use a variety of search terms to discover more about him in historical newspapers. He was always known officially as William Eggelton with that specific spelling and he had no middle name or known nickname. In some written records, the spelling of his surname changed to Eggleton so this is the first obvious spelling variation to check for. We can also see he was a private during the First World War giving another potential name to search for. Accounting for spelling variations and common mistranscriptions (such as reading text as y instead of g) by OCR, I could therefore use the following name searches for William:

William Eggelton, William Eggleton, William Egelton, William Egleton, Mr W. Eggelton, Mr W. Eggleton, Mr Eggelton, Mr Eggleton, Pte. W Eggelton, Pte. Eggleton, Private Eggelton, Private Eggleton, William Eyyelton, William Eyyleton, Will. Eggelton, Will. Eggleton, Wm Eggelton, Wm Eggleton, William E*ton, W* Eg*on

The above list is not exhaustive, showing just how many potential searches need to be carried out using a name alone. Due to the inaccuracies of OCR and the poor quality of some papers, William could be transcribed quite literally as anything. This could be Wi11ium or M!l1ie%n and anything in-between. We have to draw the line somewhere of course, so search for the most likely terms and try different words. William may not have been read correctly but Eggelton may have been. Some results could be filtered out, for example he was not known as Private Eggelton until 1914 so we can eliminate any results prior to this date. You may also wish to filter other results as you go. In the case of searching for 'Pte Eggleton', there are a lot of results regarding a Dennis or Denis Eggleton. I could therefore choose to eliminate any results using these two names.

To cover further bases when looking for articles involving William, we would need to add other details that we know about him, such as parishes and addresses. Using his timeline, some of the suggested searches would be:

Eggelton Fenny, Eggleton Fenny, Eggelton Linslade, Eggleton Linslade, Eggelton Bletchley, Eggleton Bletchley, 13 South Terrace, 46 Park Street, 46 Park St, 35 Victoria Road, 35 Victoria

Rd, Eggelton South Terrace, Eggelton Park Street, Eggelton Park St, Eggelton Victoria Road, Eggelton Victoria Rd

With regard to searching for addresses and place names, we can narrow the results down by the date we know William was residing there. For example, he is listed as living at 46 Park Street in the 1901 census but not the returns either side. Without further knowledge, we can filter the results to 1891–1911, covering the chance he may have moved shortly after the 1891 census or shortly before the 1911 census was taken. By searching for terms such as 'Eggelton Bletchley', we may also receive results for his father, Robert, who we also know was living there at the same time as William. It is recommended to search for the specific numbered address, where known, to find targeted results, but also using the road name without the number separately as this was not always given.

Looking again at the timeline gives us more ideas for specific search terms. These could include searching for his regimental numbers (most likely alongside his surname plus variations); the deaths of his parents to see if William is named in any obituary; the surnames of 'Eggelton Bowler' to look for marriage reports; using occupational terms such as 'Eggelton railway' or 'Eggelton carpenter'; and the births of his children. We could also search neighbouring addresses to see if anything noteworthy happened next door that William would have been aware of, such as a major crime or a tragic accident. We should also remember to search for William's other family members, including his wife, stepmother and sister, to see if he is mentioned.

If we are interested in finding out more generalised information about William's life rather than finding him named specifically, we could search for terms such as 'railway carpenter' and narrow the results down to Buckinghamshire county to see what articles exist about his occupation in the county at the time. We could research more into each of the parishes he resided in during his time in them to see what major changes would have affected him, and use the regiments he served with as general terms to track their activities during the dates he served with them.

As well as the search terms above, we also need to remember that they should all be carried out via each newspaper search database to ensure we have searched as many different titles as possible. Plus, the searches should be repeated in the future to look for results that have been uploaded in the meantime. At all times, different spelling variations should be checked for each term, including for addresses and occupations. You may also wish to browse newspapers held within libraries and archives if these have not yet been digitised and you are looking for a specific event. The case study above only looks at select records rather than all documentation that is held about him to simplify matters here. From the example of William Eggelton, it is easy to see how so many results are missed and how, even after all these years, I am still finding new results for my ancestors within historical newspapers today. We cannot simply type in a name and expect to find all relevant records, if any.

Chapter 14

WHERE TO FIND RELEVANT NEWSPAPER ARTICLES

We are lucky that today millions of newspaper pages are available for us to view from the comfort of our homes via the internet. Previously, historical newspapers could only be viewed by visiting archives and libraries and browsing page by page or using an annually issued index. This was very time-consuming and meant most genealogists simply did not look through them. Of those that did, the majority of relevant articles would have been missed because, as we have found out, many articles about our ancestors are about issues that we were not previously aware of. Historically, those reports that were found related to events where the dates were known and newspapers could be browsed faster, such as births, marriages and deaths.

Many newspaper articles were cut out and kept by our ancestors in a way that many people still do today and these remain in family hands. I have many of these that have been handed down to me relating to my family that have yet to appear online. Unfortunately, due to the way they have been cut from the paper, the date and title of the newspaper has been lost. When we are using newspapers as a source it is important to remember that not all have survived. Some of the short-lived titles have disappeared, as well as some larger titles such as *The Leeds Mercury* for the late 1740s.

It is not possible to provide a full list of previous and existing newspaper titles and where to find them, as the list is constantly evolving. I have, therefore, provided a link, where possible, for each website's newspaper title holding. As more are being added, it is worth checking back frequently to see which new collections have been added. The British Library has a complete list of their holdings available to download as a dataset from their Research Repository at **https://bl.iro.bl.uk**. You can search this by any term, including title and place of publication, helping you to discover what titles exist for named places and for which date ranges. This will tell you which titles are yet to be digitised and which are available online.

Jeremy Gibson's guide, *Local Newspapers 1750–1920*, is also a useful resource for uncovering provincial titles in England, Wales, the Channel Islands and the Isle of Man. You can find copies sold via some Family History Societies, as well as copies being sold second-hand online. Now in its third edition, this booklet, as well as the British Library's previous list, can be used to discover what titles existed for your ancestor's local area.

Viewing Newspapers Offline

You may find that a newspaper that you wish to view is not yet available online. Some people also simply prefer to search collections in the traditional way. It may also be the case that the relevant newspaper you wish to view is online but the page you are interested in is damaged and unreadable and you need to source another copy. Photographs often do not scan well and you may wish to see the original image. Whatever the reason, there are many places that house historical newspapers.

The British Library houses the best collection of historical national and provincial newspapers from the early seventeenth century to the present day. The collection consists of over half a million bound volumes of newspapers and 36,000 different titles at its Newsroom site in St Pancras, London. As well as British newspapers, it also holds copies originating from 190 other countries. You may still opt to visit the British Library to view the newspapers in person. Bear in mind, however, you are unlikely to be given an original newspaper copy to hold. The British Library, understandably, needs to conserve the newspapers in its care. In place of the original you may be directed to view them on microfilm or a digital facsimile. Due to its partnership with British Newspaper Archive, new newspaper editions are uploaded online every week.

Other libraries, including the National Library of Scotland and National Library of Wales, hold fantastic collections relating to their regions. Many local libraries also retain provincial papers. The collection from the National Library of Wales can be viewed online as will be discussed below, whereas the National Library of Scotland has very few titles available online thus far. You may also find national titles held at larger libraries. For example, *The Gazette* can be found at the British Library, Guildhall Library and Cambridge University Library. The Bodleian Library at Oxford also holds many early titles.

The National Archives has a good collection of transport-related newspapers. Many of these originate from different railway companies and some are cuttings of selected articles rather than the entire paper. These are not currently available to view online. Other selected newspaper articles are available to download for free; however, these are few and generally not catalogued by a person's name. Most of these come under the Ministry of Health category, with cuttings relating to workhouse management and the running of Poor Law Unions.

Most national newspapers and some provincial editions created indexes each year, which could be used by researchers. For regional newspapers preserved in local libraries, staff sometimes created their own card indexes. Both library staff and archive staff often retained clippings of particular articles in the same way that our ancestors may have done. Many of those retained by archives have been catalogued and are searchable online in their collection catalogues. While you are at the library, check to see if you can access some of the websites listed below for free. Many allow you to use subscription websites through their facilities, including, sometimes, from home using your library card.

The Gazette – www.thegazette.co.uk

As mentioned in Chapter 1, *The Gazette* refers to *The London Gazette*, *The Edinburgh Gazette* and *The Belfast Gazette*. They are all official public records of the government published by The Stationery Office and can help you to discover if your ancestor received any awards such as MBEs and OBEs, were made bankrupt or altered a coat of arms.

All editions from 1665 can be searched online via the 'search the archives' box on their homepages. After entering a keyword, you can choose to sort the results by date or by relevance. You can also filter the results by the type of notice (e.g. honours and awards or companies), location and date. You can save your searches if you wish by creating a free account. *The Dublin Gazette* can be viewed for a fee at https://newspaperarchive.com/

The British Newspaper Archive (BNA) – www.britishnewspaperarchive.co.uk

The BNA was launched in 2011 and has revolutionised the way genealogists and those with other historical interests can research newspapers. Owned by Findmypast, the website is a partnership with the British Library, created to digitise as many newspapers as possible to increase public access to them. BNA adds more titles to its website each week with updates given on its blog at **https://blog.britishnewspaperarchive.co.uk**. A complete list of all of the collections available on BNA can be found at **www.**

britishnewspaperarchive.co.uk/home/newspapertitles. This is shown in alphabetical order alongside the years that are available. Currently you can pay for a monthly, three-monthly or an annual subscription. The same newspapers are available to view via the Findmypast website at **www.findmypast.co.uk/search-newspapers** with an 'Everything' subscription.

On both BNA and Findmypast there are a select number of free newspapers available to view. These can be easily found either via the 'Free to View' link on BNA's homepage or by selecting the 'Free to View' or 'Free Today' options on Findmypast after entering a search term under the 'Article Access' dropdown button. The majority will, however, require a paid subscription to view. When you first register with BNA, you also get three free pages.

Via the homepage of BNA, you can browse by date, country, region, county, place or by their most recently added titles. Most of the time you will search using one or more keywords. This may include an ancestor's name, occupation or place of residence, among limitless other terms. After entering a search term, a list of results will be provided. Down the left-hand side are filtering options, including date, newspaper title, location, access type (free or subscription only) and the type of article, such as advertisement, family notices and illustrated. The latter are not always accurate. The filters are almost identical on Findmypast but here are placed at the top of the screen above the list of results. Both BNA and Findmypast provide an 'advanced search' option, which may be useful. This allows you to search for an exact phrase and exclude certain words as well as adjust the previous filter options. When a relevant article is found, this may be cropped and added to your family tree on Findmypast using the 'Clip' function. There is also an option on BNA to send in corrections if you find errors within the OCR transcription.

Newspapers by Ancestry – www.newspapers.com

Newspapers by Ancestry is a subscription site with options to pay per month or six months. You can choose to subscribe directly via the website or instead you can access it using an 'All Access' Ancestry membership. This website has many overlaps with the BNA; however, there are some titles that you will not find there. These include *The Guardian* and *Evening Standard* (at the time of writing) and many provincial titles. Personally, I have found many articles relating to the past seventy-five years here that are not yet available on BNA which has helped me to research my grandparents and closer relatives.

A list of their available titles can be found at **www.newspapers.com/papers**. There are currently over 29,000 although only 1,490 of these relate to the United Kingdom. An overwhelming majority relate to the

United States, with others featuring from Ireland, Canada, Australia and New Zealand. The newspapers are updated regularly with those from the current year which may help you to search for living relatives.

You can either browse by newspaper title or by keyword. You can then filter using date, location, newspaper title, category or when the newspaper was added to the online collection. The results are best viewed via a desktop browser as currently the mobile display does not show much information. You can opt to receive a search alert when a new result is uploaded. Perhaps of most use is the clippings function. This gives you the option to crop a relevant news article and save it to your Ancestry account, saving it to the right person in your tree for ease of access in the future.

Old News by MyHeritage – www.oldnews.com

MyHeritage's historical newspaper offering launched in 2024 and boasts thousands of worldwide titles. You can log in using your MyHeritage account details. The site focuses largely on newspapers from outside of Britain; however, it does offer titles such as *The Gazette* and *The Economist*. More newspapers are added to the site each month so it is worth checking back periodically. You can search by keyword, date and publication place and then you can filter by publication title. This site is best used by those researching ancestry from the United States but British updates are expected.

Welsh Newspapers Online – https://newspapers.library.wales

The website of the National Library of Wales allows free access to its digital newspaper collection. You can search by keyword and filter by title, date, article type and language (English or Welsh). You can also choose to browse by location, decade or title. The results are displayed in a list with the filtering options available on the left-hand side. The list of available newspaper titles, of which there are over 120, is available on the link above. These date from 1804 to 1919. Over 4 million of its 15 million articles are from the *Evening Express* from Cardiff. This website is an absolute must for those researching Welsh ancestry in the nineteenth century.

The National Library of Scotland – https://digital.nls.uk/scotlands-news

The National Library of Scotland is undergoing a digitisation project aiming to make some newspapers within its care accessible online. This is particularly focused on the older and more fragile newspapers within its collection. At the time of writing there are seventeen titles available, including the *Scots Courant*, *Caledonian Mercury* and *The Aberdeen New Shaver*. The website advises to check back for more progress. You can search by keyword with results presented in a long list, sortable by relevance or title. The website is not particularly user-friendly; however, the scans are very clear and easily readable.

Gale – www.gale.com/intl/primary-sources/historical-newspapers

Gale is surprisingly less known among the genealogy sector but could be a boon to your research. Via its website you can access hundreds of newspaper titles, including *The Illustrated London News*, *The Times*, *The Mirror* and *Financial Times*. Its collection of British Library newspapers also includes many regional titles. You can access Gale via selected universities and libraries and there is a feature at **https://link.gale.com/apps** to find your nearest access point. You can also access Gale from home using some library cards. Check with your local library to see if this is possible for you.

Isle of Wight County Press Archive – https://www.countypress. co.uk/newspaper-archive

For any ancestors who lived on the Isle of Wight, you may discover their stories here. You can search for free but must pay to view the pages. The *Isle of Wight County Press* has been published since 1884, with over 6,500 editions. You can search by keyword and filter by date, section (e.g. motoring or property) or choose to search only the front pages or inner pages. Family notices were initially featured on its front page until 1974, which is worth bearing in mind for your search. You can choose to subscribe for two days, seven days, thirty days or per year.

Manx National Heritage – www.imuseum.im/newspapers

If your ancestors lived on the Isle of Man, it is worth searching the digital newspaper archive of the Manx National Heritage Library. The articles date from 1792 to 1960 and at the time of writing there are forty-two titles. You can sort the results by relevance and date or choose to filter by title. Titles include the *Isle of Man Times*, *Manx Patriot* and the *Ramsey Chronicle*. The site is completely free to use and you can choose to view the entire page or only the relevant article to your search.

Nineteenth-Century Serials Edition (NCSE) – https://ncse.ac.uk/index.html

Here you can access seven titles for free. These are the *Monthly Repository* (1806–1837), *Unitarian Chronicle* (1832–1833), *Northern Star* (1838–1852),

Leader (1850–1860), *English Woman's Journal* (1858–1864), *Tomahawk* (1867–1870) and *Publishers' Circular* (1880–1890). These fascinating titles can give insight into our ancestors' political thoughts, such as Chartism in the *Northern Star* or the nineteenth-century suffragette movement in the *English Women's Journal*. You can search by keyword and sort the results by date, title or relevance. You can then opt to filter the results by year, title or item (advertisement or text).

Google News – https://news.google.co.uk

Google News has digitised a number of newspapers, largely relating to the United States and Canada. There are a number of British newspapers that may be of interest, including the *Edinburgh Weekly Journal* and *The London Evening Advertiser*. The range of available titles can be seen at **https://news.google.com/newspapers**. This is unlikely to be a genealogist's first port of call when researching historical newspapers; however, it could provide a lead if your ancestor emigrated, even if only for a short period. As many copies also go up to the twenty-first century, the papers may also help you to trace living relatives who live abroad. The advanced search enables you to filter by publication date, title and language.

Internet Archive – https://archive.org/details/newspapers

The Internet Archive has a growing popularity among genealogists who are beginning to recognise the potential of this free site. Among collections, including books, videos and audio recordings, are a good number of newspapers from around the world. You can filter results by keyword, year and language. British titles are mostly from the last thirty years, including select issues of *The Times, Banbury Cake, Cannock Chronicle* and *The Barry & Penarth Gem*.

Hathi Trust – www.hathitrust.org

The Hathi Trust is a fantastic free resource for written material. While its strengths lie in historical books, it does have several journals and some newspapers from Britain. These include *The London Gazette, The Gardeners' Chronicle and Agricultural Gazette, The Statist* and *The Christian*. Issues of *The Gentleman's Magazine* are also available to view for free. You can choose to search by title, full text and subject.

Other

Some newspapers allow access to their archives via their own websites. These include *The Times* **www.thetimes.com/archive**, *The Scotsman*

www.scotsman.com/archive, *The Spectator* **https://archive.spectator. co.uk** and *The Guardian* and *Observer* **www.theguardian.com/gnm-archive** as well as some provincial publications. Many charge a fee; however, some are free to access. Some of these papers can be accessed from alternative sites, such as *The Guardian* via Newspapers by Ancestry and *The Times* via Gale. You can also visit **www.onlinenewspapers.com** for links to the websites of individual newspaper titles. It is worth checking whether a newspaper is available elsewhere for free before paying for access. You may also want to check out Last Chance to Read **www.lastchancetoread.com.** This has not been updated for a while and requires payment, but you may find articles here that are not available anywhere else.

Chapter 15

NON-BRITISH NEWSPAPERS

Many of us have ancestors who travelled overseas. Whether this was a permanent move or only temporary, you may find that they appear in the foreign press. Even if your ancestors moved permanently overseas they may still feature in the British press, with many families sending details of births, marriages and deaths to newspapers back in their original home country. Obituaries of ancestors who died overseas often include information about their time in Britain, including when and where they were born and when they emigrated. You may also find crimes committed by British migrants featuring in the British press. Even if your ancestors never resided overseas, it can be enlightening to see how some events, such as certain battles, were reported in contrast to British publications.

The British newspaper industry was initially ahead of other countries in terms of its existence and technology. Even when other countries began to publish their own newspapers, many were largely extracts taken from London editions. You may, therefore, be disappointed to find little mention of overseas ancestors being named in the early days of the foreign printing press. Newspapers were often introduced overseas by British travellers to the colony. Within just three months of the first immigrant ship arriving in New Zealand in 1839, the first newspaper, *The New Zealand Gazette*, was founded.

The first continuously published title to last within the United States is deemed to be *The Weekly Boston News-Letter* whose first edition appeared on 24 April 1704. This lasted until 1776. *The New York Gazette* appeared in 1725, with the last edition printed in 1744. The first successful daily newspaper published in the United States was the *Pennsylvania Packet and Daily Advertiser* in 1784, followed by the *Daily Advertiser* of New York in 1785. Canada's first newspaper did not appear until 1752 in the form of *The Halifax Gazette*.

The Sydney Gazette was the first newspaper published in Australia in 1803 and was an official publication. Other official newspapers followed in Hobart (*Van Diemen's Land Gazette and General Advertiser*) and Derwent (*The Derwent Star*), both in 1810. It was not until the 1830s that a comparable newspaper press began to emerge in the country. The first daily newspaper containing local news appeared in 1840 when *The Sydney Morning Herald* moved from publishing weekly to every day. It was not until 1891 that the first daily national newspaper was established in the form of *Daily Commercial News*.

India was ahead of the times, compared to most countries. *Hicky's Bengal Gazette* dates back to 1780 and was founded by an Irishman named James Hicky. The newspaper was somewhat controversial in its views but was especially popular with British soldiers and other Britons who worked around Kolkata. Other businessmen spotted an opportunity to develop their own newspapers following its success and many others began to spring up. As happened in Britain, many early titles did not last long.

The first recognisable newspaper in Ireland was published in Cork in 1649 entitled *The Irish Monthly Mercury*. Yet it was not until the mid-1800s that the Irish newspaper industry really took off. Many were of a specific religious persuasion, such as *The Protestant Watchman and Lurgan Gazette* and *The Catholic Telegraph*. The British Newspaper Archive and Findmypast have a large range of Irish newspapers, including *The Cork Daily Herald*, Dublin's *Evening Herald* and *The Irish Times*. You may also choose to visit Irish Newspaper Archive at **www.irishnewsarchive.com** and National Library of Ireland at **www.nli.ie/collections/our-collections/newspapers**.

Some of the websites below featuring foreign newspapers overlap from those containing British publications seen in Chapter 14. There are also many others that are different and only hold newspapers from overseas. The countries have been chosen due to the likelihood of a British person having emigrated there, such as the high numbers that moved to the United States and Australia. If your ancestor lived in a country not mentioned below, use a search engine to see what newspaper archives are available online. Bear in mind the country that your ancestor resided in and search the most relevant websites below accordingly. Also remember that transcriptions remain in the native language and are not translated into English.

Newspapers by Ancestry – www.newspapers.com

There are currently thirteen countries with newspapers featured on Newspapers.com: Australia, Canada, Timor-Leste, Indonesia, Ireland, New

Zealand, Panama, Papua New Guinea, Philippines, Samoa, Thailand, the United Kingdom and the United States. The greatest number of titles featured here relate to the United States. Some countries, including Indonesia and Timor-Leste, currently only have one title available – namely *Berita Repoeblik Indonesia* and *A Voz de Timor*. You can choose to browse by publication country at **www.newspapers.com/browse**. As well as the United States, the site has a good number of titles from Canada and Australia.

Old News by MyHeritage – www.oldnews.com

Old News is one of the more recent additions to the digitised newspaper front. There are newspapers from the United States, Canada and Australia as well as others, including Denmark, Germany, Austria and Norway. You will find foreign titles on here that you cannot find elsewhere and is particularly useful if your ancestors travelled to or from America or elsewhere in Europe. There are millions of results from the United States. You can log in using your MyHeritage account details.

Gale – www.gale.com/intl/primary-sources/historical-newspapers

Gale's overseas collection comprises of *Liberty*, *New York Herald*, *Cleveland Daily Herald* and many other American titles. There are also many American periodicals held by the American Antiquarian Society available to view. Accessing the American newspapers via Gale is the same as with British papers meaning you can access the site from selected universities and libraries with a feature at **https://link.gale. com/apps** to find your nearest access point. Gale can also be accessed from home using some library cards – check with your local library to see if this is possible for you.

Chronicling America – https://chroniclingamerica.loc.gov

For those of you looking for ancestors who immigrated to (or emigrated from) the United States, this free website will be of great use to you with titles dating 1756–1963. You can search by keyword and narrow results down by state, date range and language. You can choose to sort the results by relevance, date, state and title. Via this website there is a directory at **https://chroniclingamerica.loc.gov/search/titles** of titles published in the USA from 1690 to the present day, but be aware that some have yet to be digitised.

Trove – https://trove.nla.gov.au

Trove is a collaboration between the National Library of Australia and a huge range of its partners from across the country, including its principal partners – the State Libraries of New South Wales, Queensland, Western Australia and Victoria. The website lets you freely browse and search the historical newspapers of Australia. Enter a keyword in the search box on the homepage and select 'Newspapers & Gazettes' from the dropdown list on the right-hand side. The results can be sorted by relevance or date and filtered by state, title, category (e.g. family notices, advertising), date, illustration type (e.g. photo, map) and word count. Newspapers are still being digitised and uploaded to the present day.

Papers Past – https://paperspast.natlib.govt.nz

Papers Past is run by the National Library of New Zealand with newspapers from 1839 to 1950. Newspapers can be browsed by title, region or year. You can also search by keyword with options to filter by date and title. The results can then be sorted by relevance, date, title, article title or content type. A complete list of available titles can be seen at **https://paperspast.natlib.govt.nz/newspapers/all** showing the region they are from and the dates they were published. Via the 'About' page, you can discover recently updated content as well as what is upcoming.

Google News – https://news.google.co.uk

Google News' strength lies in overseas newspapers, of which there are hundreds. The titles it holds can be seen at **https://news.google.com/newspapers** and largely includes newspapers from the United States and Canada such as *The Calgary Weekly Herald*, *The Iowa Age* and *Las Vegas Times*. There are also a number of titles from France, such as *La Gazette du Nord*, and Australia, such as *The Sydney Morning Herald*.

Internet Archive – https://archive.org/details/newspapers

The Internet Archive boasts a huge range of free foreign newspapers. There are offerings from Asia, including *The China Weekly Review* and *The Hong Kong Daily Press*; Italy, such as *La Patria del Friuli* and *Cittadino Italiano*; and Ukraine, such as *Svoboda*. By heading directly to the link given above, you can then choose to enter a search term, filter by year, language and media type.

Hathi Trust – www.hathitrust.org

The Hathi Trust is an easy-to-use, free resource full of information. Enter your search term and then select 'Newspaper' under the 'Original Format' option on the left-hand side of the screen. Other options include books, directories and journals, which you may also choose to peruse. The largest collection of foreign newspapers originates from the United

States, including general titles, such as *The Daily Californian*, as well as more specialist titles such as *The Tobacco Worker* and *The Chicago Banker*. Other countries that are represented include Canada, with titles including *The Missiskoui Standard*, Germany with titles such as *Allgemeine Zeitung*, and Japan with *The Japan Daily Mail*.

Other

There are a wide variety of websites available showcasing overseas newspapers. Some are available via the newspaper website themselves through an online archive, whereas others are via a hosting website. Some are free, whereas others have a charge. If your ancestor travelled abroad, whether temporarily or permanently, it is worth browsing the newspapers for the country they relocated to. There are also rarer cases where British tourists are named in local foreign press, usually if they were involved in an accident or crime.

Many foreign websites offer a function to translate their webpages to English. Where this is not available you can usually do this via your browser. Be aware, however, that images, including those of newspaper pages, cannot be translated. Some other examples of websites you may find useful include:

- **gazette.gc.ca** is the website for the official newspaper of the Government of Canada known as the *Canada Gazette*
- **https://anno.onb.ac.at** hosts a range of Austrian newspapers
- **https://tidningar.kb.se** for Swedish newspapers dating back to 1645 via the National Library of Sweden
- **www.bnf.fr/en/gallica-bnf-digital-library** Gallica is the digital library of the French National Library
- **http://emeroteca.braidense.it** currently has access to 960 Italian newspapers
- **www.elephind.com** describes itself as 'like Google but for newspapers', allowing you to search for articles from a variety of online sources. A majority of these are US-based but other countries do feature, such as New Zealand

Chapter 16

AFTERWORD

It is difficult to think of what life would have been like in our ancestors' time. Reading newspapers can truly help place them in history. We can understand what artwork was recently painted, what types of vehicle were on the road, what local crime levels were like, what people wore, what products were available for them to purchase and what military activity was occurring. They can give us an overall contemporary context in a way that no other source can.

Obviously, the biggest advantage of newspapers is where we are able to find specific mentions of our forebears. You will likely have ancestors who are named numerous times in various circumstances. By piecing together multiple articles, we can really start to gather a true picture of our ancestors, their characters and their lives.

There is little doubt that newspapers are among one of the fastest-growing genealogical sources of our time thanks to digitisation, OCR and increased awareness. While we must remember to be cautious of using newspapers due to their limitations, including their reliability and transcription issues, we must also be careful to extract as much information from the source as we can. When we have done this, we must also back up the information with another source where possible.

You may find newspapers useful to break down a brick wall thanks to an appearance in a births' column or the mention of a parent's name in a court transcript. The main aim of this book, however, was to encourage readers to discover more about their ancestors' characters through newspaper articles. You can discover details about people long ago that you simply cannot find elsewhere. Part of the joy of using a newspaper online search database is the excitement and surprise that comes with the results that are uncovered; news stories that our forebears undoubtedly thought would have been long forgotten by now.

Whatever stories you unearth, remember our ancestors were human like us. They made mistakes, they had accidents and they would not always have made the right choices. You may wish to think about how you or your close family members would be remembered if the only source that survived for their descendants to research them by was newspapers. This highlights that while newspapers are a crucial genealogical source, they are not the only source. Use them as you would any other to complement your research and do your ancestors justice by discovering as much about their story as you can.

You may, at times, feel frustrated with your research, feeling as though you are struggling to uncover your ancestors' stories. This is not uncommon and there is no shame in taking a break and returning to your research at a later date. During this time, further titles may have been digitised and released and these new updates may give you the breakthrough you were waiting for. Take time to consider different spelling variants you could try, different search terms and different websites that may hold alternative titles.

I sincerely hope this book has helped you to discover more about your family tree. I search for my ancestors and distant cousins in historical newspapers most days and am always surprised at what I am still uncovering after all these years. A good search result often makes my day and I truly hope it is the same for you. Never give up as you will find that with practice, your research and detective skills will constantly improve. Good luck!

INDEX

Dear Reader,

We hope you have enjoyed this book, but why not share your views on social media? You can also follow our pages to see more about our other products: facebook.com/penandswordbooks or follow us on X @penswordbooks

You can also view our products at www.pen-and-sword.co.uk (UK and ROW) or www.penandswordbooks.com (North America).

To keep up to date with our latest releases and online catalogues, please sign up to our newsletter at: www.pen-and-sword.co.uk/newsletter

If you would like a printed catalogue with our latest books, then please email: enquiries@pen-and-sword.co.uk or telephone: 01226 734555 (UK and ROW) or email: uspen-and-sword@casematepublishers.com or telephone: (610) 853-9131 (North America).

We respect your privacy and we will only use personal information to send you information about our products.

Thank you!